BUSINESS
BALANCE
& Bliss

BUSINESS
BALANCE
& Bliss

HOW THE B³ METHOD CAN
TRANSFORM YOUR CAREER AND LIFE

 AMY VETTER

QUICKSTART TRAINING, INC.
MASON, OHIO

© 2017 Amy Vetter

Published by
QuickStart Training, Inc.
Mason, OH

     Publisher's Cataloging-in-Publication Data
     Vetter, Amy.

     Business, balance, and bliss : how the B^3 method can transform your career and life / Amy Vetter. – Mason, OH : QuickStart Training, Inc., 2017.

     p. ; cm.

     ISBN13: 978-0-9980144-0-1

     1. Success in business. 2. Success. I. Title.

     HF5386.V47 2017
     650.1—dc23   2017935982

Project coordination by Jenkins Group, Inc.
www.BookPublishing.com

Front cover design by Mary Rose Lytle
Interior design by Brooke Camfield

Printed in the United States of America
21 20 19 18 17 • 5 4 3 2 1

To my husband Rob, and my sons Jagger and Austin,
without your love, caring, and support,
this book and my own transformation
would not have been possible.

CONTENTS

ACKNOWLEDGMENTS

I would like to acknowledge all the people who have contributed to this book, either with their stories and suggestions, or their support in getting this message out to people who are in need of change in their lives.

First, I would like to acknowledge the women who served as my role models and support throughout different times in my life. My mother and grandmother provided an example of strength and independence that inspired me to never doubt that I can achieve what I set my mind to. My girlfriends, Stephanie Cable and Jenna McHugh have served as my confidants and mutual support, throughout my career.

Next, I would like to thank all the people who have contributed to this book in some way, whether through their stories, edits, or reviews. You have helped make my ideas meaningful to readers. Thanks to Sharna Brockett, Kimberly Ellison-Taylor, Tom Hood, Peter Karpas, Greg Kyte, Mary Lytle, Vivian Maza, Misty Megia, Jeannie Ruesch, Matthew Solan, and Ambra Wellbeloved.

Last and most important, I could not have written this book without the love and support of my husband Rob and my sons Jagger and Austin. They make every day an adventure and worth living. I am so fortunate and grateful for the family I have and for living an authentic life with them.

Thanks to everyone who has chosen to begin this journey by taking the first step toward work-life harmony with the B³ Method. My hope is that the stories, my own and others, and the research in this book will inspire you to think about these ideas and begin to incorporate them into your own life. I look forward to hearing your stories about how you have applied this methodology and are working toward transforming your career and life.

INTRODUCING THE B³ METHOD

Rethinking how we strive for work-life harmony

When you think about a major moment in your career, what stands out? For many people, it usually involves any series of firsts: the first job interview, the first job offer, the first raise, and the first promotion.

I have enjoyed my series of memorable firsts, but the single moment for me occurred much later in my career. It changed not only how I conduct my business but also how I manage my life, family, and livelihood.

I was thirty-two. I worked at a well-respected accounting firm in South Florida and had just made partner that day. My office was typical of any senior-level employee: big black chair; polished desk; and walls covered with certificates, plaques, and framed pictures of my family within easy view.

One of the managing partners in the firm knocked on my door and entered. Before I could say anything, he extended his hand along with an award-winning smile. "Congratulations!" he said.

My entire professional life had been building up to this moment. The years of learning about business through witnessing my mother's business successes and failures; the hours of college lectures; internships; entry into corporate America; launching my own business; moving up the ranks; and industry praise, promotions, bonuses, new titles, bigger offices—these were the steps I had taken to achieve this singular moment. I felt I had finally arrived at the summit. Partner. Recognition. Success. To be a leader in an accounting firm.

But his next sentence changed everything.

He said, "I love knowing who I will retire with."

I lost my breath.

Not because I was surprised or excited or feeling euphoric about becoming a partner.

It was just the opposite. I felt almost complete and utter despair.

While he was so gleeful about the certainty of knowing that he would work side by side with me for the next thirty-plus years, it suddenly struck me. I had not reached the top; instead, I'd reached the end of the line. This was it? Yes, being named a partner came with more money and other fringe benefits as well as its share of opportunity like taking an active role in business decisions and company direction. It was what I had worked toward for so many years. It drove me; it gave me a goal to achieve. Instead the only thought flashing through my mind was—now what? What would my goals be now? What would I work toward?? What else did I have left to do? Was this the meaning of "success"?

Up until this point, I had formulated a personal strategy for business since a young age that I had cultivated through years of observations and personal trial and error. I thought I understood what I needed to do to excel in business whether just starting out, seeking to move up in a company, expanding my leadership skills, wanting to strike out on my own, or just reaching my full potential. Outside the office, I also had so much to be thankful for: great husband, great children, and a great home.

I began to question everything.

Now that I was here, I realized it wasn't enough. My strategy was somehow flawed. Yes, I was successful in the classic sense, and probably by anybody else's standard, but why wasn't I happy at the moment I should have been? Why wasn't it enough? What was wrong?

Around this time, I began to see a therapist and decided to go to his office and meet with him rather than celebrating the news with champagne and dinner. I needed to find out why I felt so bad after receiving what I believed to be the ultimate professional reward.

My therapist and I worked together to find a solution during the times we met. He believed that the promotion had revealed something else that was glaringly absent from my life: balance.

"Your reaction was your body's way of telling you that you need to deal with things," he said.

And he was right.

I was not taking care of my well-being. All my energy was directed outward to work and family, and it created a drastic imbalance. I realized at that time that without proper balance, I couldn't really reach my potential in business. That meant dealing with all aspects of it, the good and the bad— how to deal with negative people, how to stand up for your values, how to confront bullies and intimidation, and how to overcome mistakes (and I have made plenty) without all your hard work and confidence unraveling.

Without that balance, you cannot obtain bliss, or sustained happiness. And without either, you cannot excel in business or in life. I realized the foundation for success consisted of these three levels, each connected with the other. Without one, the others will ultimately fail.

It wasn't that I felt I didn't deserve the partnership. I did deserve it. I knew I had fully earned the recognition and had the proven track record to show for it. Instead, I realized that what had driven me through all those years was the goal of becoming a partner; it kept me motivated, and I had assumed attaining it would create happiness in my career. I was hiding behind this goal and never really listening to myself or taking time to acknowledge what would actually make me happy as a person.

That defining moment in my life helped wake me up and begin the journey to happiness in business and in life. Whether it is choosing your career path, overcoming insecurities, finding your voice of authority, or navigating the turbulent waters of corporate America, you need to recognize the triangular effect of **Business, Balance, and Bliss**. So often we—me included—are programmed to believe that we have to give up something in order to gain. This is simply not true. In fact, you need to invest more, not less, into other aspects of your life to find complete fulfillment. Happiness extends beyond the office. To excel in business, we have to excel outside of it, and vice versa.

The Struggles of Work-Life Harmony

We hear a lot about work-life balance. It's a nice catchall phrase that attempts to explain the daily attention we place on both our work and home life. Can you give equal attention to a career and a family?

However, I prefer the phrase work-life *harmony* because it invokes the idea that you should enjoy work and enjoy life at the rhythm that makes the best sense for your life—with no pressure or stress.

Work-life harmony is a constant dance between the worlds of work and family—but the two can coexist. Your business can help provide for your family. Having a family can be the motivation to excel in business, and you can find ways to fulfill your passions and dreams.

I faced this dilemma throughout my life. I thought I had to make hard choices, instead of asking, "Why does it have to be this way?"

My awakening was the beginning of my transformation. Within a year, I left the partnership and went out on my own again with my own accounting practice. My goal was now to reinvent my philosophy and how I approached both my business and my life, rather than being consumed by work.

I stepped back and examined how I had approached business and what worked and didn't. I looked at how my own productivity and time management (as well as those of my employees) translated into actual progress.

I revisited my own family business roots. I studied how others, both men and women, approached their business roles and why some succeeded and others struggled. I looked closely at how people tried to balance raising a family with building a career while also maintaining their home, relationships, and own well-being—and without sacrificing one for the others. My self-reflection offered an awakening to what was really important to me and how to have a more fulfilling life.

It has been a long journey with plenty of ups and downs and sideways along the way, but soon I crafted a new philosophy built around what I believe are the three areas for all-around success. I call them the three Bs: Business, Balance, and Bliss, or more simply, the B³ Method.

The B³ Method can help you navigate the common challenges that we face in the workplace, no matter your current path. Whether you're just starting out or are a seasoned manager or an experienced entrepreneur, the B³ Method is meant to help you reach your potential as a business leader and to help you adopt the habits you need to stay healthy in your regular life.

In this book, I will show you how to apply the B³ Method to address three key areas that I believe everyone in business faces at some time. These include:

1. **How to be more present and productive (chapter 3)**

2. **How to find and maintain confidence and tame the ego (chapter 4)**

3. **How to build personal connections (chapter 5)**

So whether you are a small business owner launching your dream or someone who wants to break through the barriers of corporate America, the B³ Method was developed to help you.

But first, let's look at the three Bs of the B³ Method, how they work, and how they rely on each other.

BUSINESS

"Business" can be a broad concept because business can refer to the nature of your business (What kind of business do you do?), the type of industry ("Who does your business serve?"), or the status of your business ("How is your business going?").

The Business part of the B³ Method is all of this and much more. It is about how you pursue your professional goals as well as face and overcome the numerous challenges along the way. Everyone has problems at some time. But so often we don't know how to deal with them, which ends up hurting our business *and* our personal lives. No matter how much we succeed, we always feel we fall short in some way.

Take my mother, for example. She would be considered a business pioneer today. She started her business in the 1980s during a time when men still dominated corporate America. Even after all the feminist movements and women's rights were in place, a woman's role was still mostly designated to lower-level positions. I saw my mom as unique—she was "The Boss."

She opened a franchise maid service in the Cincinnati area that soon grew to other locations. She was an active networker, hand shaker, and dealmaker.

Despite her many strengths, however, my mother often struggled with running the mundane, but necessary, day-to-day, back-end financial side of the business. She was often trapped by the lack of technology of the day as well.

My mother's business consisted of maids, but they were not always an easy staff to manage. They had to wear proper uniforms and show up on time and go into people's homes. With so many cleaning jobs happening during any average day, it was tough to monitor productivity and scheduling, especially with all the manual processes.

Orders were taken over the phone, work orders for the maids were provided on paper—which houses to go to, what work needed to be done, and at what time. My mom then assigned the various jobs to the staff. Because it was rare to have time to visit a house and look at what needed to be done when a new customer called, bidding jobs over the phone was an educated guess.

Much of her energy was spent in the execution of her business operations, while the paper side got behind. She relied on her tax accountant to provide financials, because there was no accounting system available at the time to have at her office. She only received a snapshot of the finances every six months after the accountant prepared the financial statements; therefore, she never really knew how she did from day to day.

Hence my mother, like so many other business owners and workers of her time, struggled with work-related stress that often affected her well-being—long hours at the office and trying to keep customers and employees happy. Because everything was paper based, communication was tough, which made it difficult to establish the real-time, ongoing relationships that were needed in and out of the office. Even with her success, there were many times when she did not feel fulfilled by her work.

Do these issues sound familiar?

Fast-forward a generation and even though technology has come a long way we still face the same problems.

How we conduct business has evolved (and is always evolving); the stressful impact of work on us personally remains a constant. It doesn't matter what your chosen profession or your position. Everyone faces challenges at one time or another, and they can have a tremendous impact on our lives, health, and career. These challenges keep us from being happy and healthy and more productive.

There are resources available that teach you how to be a better leader, how to motivate people to help them reach their potential, and even that offer advice on how to succeed in business, but most resources do not address the core concerns that everyone encounters in business. Without addressing these areas, you will never be truly fulfilled, happy, or able to reach your potential.

BALANCE

"Balance" is the physical or mental outlet (or sometimes both) that you need in life. It is a way to separate the topsy-turvy business world from your personal life, but you can also utilize Balance to help you during challenging Business times.

Balance is the epicenter of the B³ Method from which everything else revolves. The next chapter goes into more detail about the importance of Balance and how to choose yours, but the point here is that you need to invest time in yourself just as much as you do your Business. It's that important. I know we may feel guilty about taking any time for ourselves, especially when raising a family. I was like that for a long time. Any "me" time simply made me feel like I was being selfish. I get that. But you have to feed your body and mind to function better at home and in the office. So don't feel guilty. Remember, you cannot be at your best if you don't see yourself as a priority. Balance is a constant reminder that you need to come first.

BLISS

Has this ever happened to you? You attend a two-day corporate retreat where the agenda is to help everyone develop stronger personal skills. Motivational speakers talk about how coworkers can better communicate with each other. You participate in role-playing scenarios and team-building exercises. You are shown how to identify your strengths and weakness and how to be more productive and happy in the workplace. You talk about things like growth, ability, and potential. You discuss how to set goals, how to achieve them, and why nothing is too big to take on if you really want it.

How do you feel by the end? No doubt, full of adrenaline and ready to take on any challenge. You are ready to make a lasting positive change in your life. You head back to your life with a comet-like gusto.

After all, you have spent hours listening and talking about how to improve yourself and reach your potential, and who doesn't want to do that?

But what ultimately happens?

You get home and immediately fall back into your normal life patterns and work routine. Sure, you might implement some of the tips and strategies you learned during your motivational weekend, but soon your enthusiasm wanes, you leave everything you learned behind, and you are right back where you began. All that time and energy was for nothing.

It's deflating, isn't it? We find the passion and desire to embrace new things and make improvements in our lives, but then cannot keep the momentum.

So what goes wrong? Why do we find a desire to embrace change and improve ourselves, but then have such a difficult time with execution?

It's an all too familiar problem that everyone (me included) has faced—how do you maintain your momentum for change? How do you get back on track if you have lost your way?

That is where the third part of the B³ Method—"Bliss"—comes into play.

Bliss is how you maintain your newfound Balance. Bliss encompasses tips and advice on how to stay on track and focused so you can let your Balance do its job of providing you with work-life harmony and happiness. Bliss helps you:

- Continue what you've learned

- Get back on track

- Revisit your Balance to ensure it still works for you

At the end of each chapter, I offer two supporting tools. The first is **B³ Basics**, which offers a summary of the chapter's key points to use as a quick reference. The second is **B³ Brainstorming** where you can make notes and record your thoughts in real-time at the end of each chapter about how you may implement the B³ Method into your life from the stories and research you read.

Business, Balance, and Bliss. They all work together to accomplish the same goal: A new way to obtain work-life harmony. You know where your troubles lie and where you need help. Let's get started so that you can begin your journey to find solutions that work in your life. First up, you must discover your Balance.

2

FINDING YOUR BALANCE

Invest in yourself—devote more time to "me" time

When someone says, "balance" what comes to mind? Equality? Two sides of a scale that are evenly weighted? The center of opposites like black and white, up and down, good and evil?

These are all accurate in the classic definition of balance. In terms of the B³ Method, balance is not about making everything even; instead, it's a means from which to build and grow.

The way today's business environment is set up often makes it a challenge to find time in our lives for anything other than work. How easy is it to get into the work-home-dinner-bed routine and repeat it every day? The weekends are about catching up—household chores, family obligations, and other commitments. Then the cycle begins again on Monday.

You need Balance in your life—for yourself, your family, and your career.

Balance, as part of the B³ Method, is not about ensuring you find more time to devote to your life, with an already full schedule—although certain aspects like spouses, children, and family are all equally important, of course. Rather it's about reallocating time to yourself: "me" time.

It can be exercise or music, or it could be painting, sculpting, arts and crafts, poetry, expressive writing, photography, drama, furniture making, knitting, cooking, and even dancing. It can be a hobby like coin collecting, model building, video games, board games, or card playing.

Balance is an investment in you. If you give your mind and body the resources to rest, grow, and expand, you will be better in all aspects of your life including your business and home life.

Yet, one of the main obstacles to obtaining Balance is not necessarily finding the time, but in recognizing that our idea of "balance" has morphed into something artificial. Balance is treated as an option instead of a necessity.

Part of the problem is that we lose sight of the value of taking care of ourselves. We have lowered the bar so much that true me time is almost non-existent. Sure, we might burn off stress with the occasional run or aerobics class, or we take periodic "personal" days, which is a way to give ourselves a twenty-four-hour vacation.

But these are temporary fixes, a quick period where you can catch your breath and recharge before diving right back into it again.

The result: You keep working and living the same way, at the same pace and getting the same results. Your personal scale resembles a seesaw where one side gets too heavy and then you have to switch to the other side until that is heavier, and then you go back and forth. The scales are never equal.

We may have a distorted vision of what Balance entails, but the workplace further blurs it despite any employer's good intentions.

In today's business climate, leaders want to create sustainable workforces where employees don't become burned out and ineffective. After all, studies have shown that happy workers are not only more productive, but they are also less likely to leave for greener pastures.

Stressed and burned out people are more cynical, lack efficacy, and are less motivated to succeed. Even business owners have fallen victim to this.

However, the business culture's solution to "balance" is to help people be in the office less—but not necessarily work less. Their solutions are to offer work-from-home days, come in and leave early, or work half days here and there. The thinking is that this provides some separation from work and life, and in this way, it supposedly provides balance. But flexibility in work just means you are doing work in a different way. You are not really balancing your work and life—just your work. This is why you need to go outside your place of business to find your Balance.

Why Do You Need Balance?

Your Balance can help with the three main areas of business success. Your Balance can make you:

- Happier and healthier

- A better thinker

- A better worker

Here is a look at these in more detail.

Happiness and Health

If you are not happy in your work, then you will not be successful. It's as simple as that. People want to do their best and be appreciated for their efforts. But so often it is up to you to create your work happiness. Some innovative companies make an effort to invest in employee happiness because they understand the return on their investment—more productivity and lower turnover.

Research backs this up—happy workers are better workers. A 2015 University of Warwick-led study discovered that employee happiness was associated with a 12 percent increase in productivity. On the other side of the coin, unhappy workers were 10 percent less productive.[1] If you are not happy and do not feel appreciated, not only will it affect your well-being and performance, but you are also much more likely to throw in the towel sooner and leave for another job with the hope that you will find happiness there.

But happiness occurs from within. Yes, business is not always fun, and there may be jobs where you simply cannot find satisfaction, but for the most part, your happiness depends on you. To be successful and enjoy your work—even when things are in disarray—you must find your own happiness. This is key to being in business.

Work can make you sick if you are not careful. Fatigue and stress are the foundation of overworked Americans, and both can have tremendous impacts on your health. In fact, it may increase your risk of early death.

Researchers publishing in *The Lancet* examined the connection between working hours and heart attack and stroke risk in more than 1 million people. They adjusted for existing health issues, such as smoking, alcohol consumption, high blood pressure, diabetes, and high cholesterol. The results showed that people who worked more than fifty-five hours weekly had a 13 percent greater risk of a heart attack and a 33 percent higher risk of stroke compared with workers who stuck to a traditional thirty-five- to forty-hour workweek.[2]

You should never have to sacrifice health for success, but so often we have trouble separating them. If the way you conduct your business affects your wellness, not only are you putting your health at risk, but it can also affect all other aspects of your life—your spouse, family, and kids. Again, business is important, and you want to succeed, but it is no reason to sacrifice health.

Better Thinker and Worker

Your Balance is not necessarily about the end result—but rather about the process. When you are engaged in activities that support your Balance, your brain gets stimulated much like a muscle being put through an intense workout.

How your brain reacts to Balance, however, is not so clear. Neuroscientists long believed that creativity came only from one hemisphere of your brain. But scientists, publishing in the journal *PLOS One*, discovered that we use both sides when we're engaged in something creative.[3] In fact, the consensus is that creativity does not involve a single brain region but is a vast team effort of multiple areas with the entire brain network working together at times and independent at others.

Yet, what appears to be clearer is the effect of creativity on your brain. What changes when you work on creating something? Neuroscience is as vast and complex as the brain itself, but one way creativity can change your thinking process is with your executive functions. These are cognitive skills, such as critical analysis, reasoning, problem solving, planning, working memory, and how you think about concepts.

Why is this important? These are the same brain skills you need to access on any given day in business. Big-picture planning meetings? Crisis with a client? A project that has hit a roadblock? These are situations when you need to tap into your best thinking, and your creative outlet can assist you in developing this "muscle" in your brain and help enhance how you confront situations and solve problems.

Your Balance can have a wide appeal in business. Besides the extra mental stimulus and expanding your executive functions, it can support and improve other aspects of how you conduct your work and collaborate with others.

Using music as an example, Peter Spellman has studied the powerful corollaries between business and music. In his book, *Indie Business Power*, he asked professional musicians about how their musical skills and experience had translated to business success. Here are a few of their responses:

- "Self-discipline"

- "Attention to detail"

- "Quick mental processing"

- "Persistence and focus"

- "Confidence and self-esteem"

- "Adaptability"

- "Teamwork and collaboration"

- "Problem solving"

- "Ability to strike compromise among diverse personalities"

- "Strong work ethic"[4]

Sounds wonderful, doesn't it? What businessperson wouldn't want to improve any one of these?

Both Warren Buffett and Bill Gates are longtime bridge players and use the game to provide some separation from their daily work. Both have commented on how the games stimulate strategic thinking and that they feel benefits in their careers because of playing it.

Buffett has commented that bridge has "got to be the best intellectual exercise out there. You're seeing through new situations every ten minutes. In the stock market, you don't base your decisions on what the market is doing but on what you think is rational. Bridge is about weighing gain-loss ratio. You're doing calculations all the time."

A colleague of mine, Peter Karpas, has worked for decades as a business leader and is an experienced marketer for many Fortune 500 companies. His creative outlets are comics as well as video and board games—throwbacks to his youth. He not only plays them for relaxation but also is involved in several groups that meet weekly to play these games or interact.

On the surface, it may seem that something like playing games is trivial—as your mom might have preached, "You are wasting your time with those video games!"—but Karpas has found many parallels between his gaming and his business.

"There is no question that my hobbies have made me a better business leader," he says. "For one, each one requires a different way of thinking, so I've learned a real variety of ways to tackle a problem. For instance, I am convinced that playing video games taught me the value of the experimentation process and also taught me to be comfortable with the failure aspect of it."

In video games, he notes, you try something and frequently it doesn't work, so you fail. But then you just try again, try something different, and eventually—through experimentation and practice—you succeed. In video games, failure is no big deal, because you can try another alternative the next time. Karpas finds that this exercise has made it easier for him to accept failure when it occurs when he tries something in business, as long as it is part of the big-picture process of succeeding in the long term.

Even his exposure to alternative worlds offers real-world lessons. His comic book hobby has helped him understand that the world he lives in is not the world of everyone else. Cincinnati is not like Los Angeles. Los Angeles is not like Dallas. Dallas is not like Boston.

"Having exposure to things outside my typical sphere expands my thinking and reminds me to ask customers about things rather than think I already know them. It helps me be much more customer focused."

Find *Your* Balance

For some people, finding Balance is quite easy. For others, it can be a journey of self-discovery. That was my case. I found my Balance during a time of great difficulty.

I developed a thyroid issue when I was pregnant with my son that lasted for a year after his birth. My thyroid basically shut down—my heart rate was out of control, my body heat shot up like a volcano, and my throat felt constricted like I couldn't swallow and like it was going to prevent me from breathing. I was prescribed beta-blockers and thyroid medicine to keep it under control, but they only did so much.

I was miserable, in pain, and it affected every part of my life: my role as a new mom, wife, and businesswoman.

Around this time, my doctor said I was not able to continue the physical fitness activity that I had enjoyed in the past because it would get my heart rate up. So, my only option would be going to yoga, and a gentle one at that. I reluctantly went to a beginner's yoga class looking for something physical that I could do at the time and that would make me feel better.

At first, I was one of those yoga nonbelievers. I had tried it before and thought it was, well, silly. In fact, I remember laughing to myself through every bend and twist when I had tried it years earlier. I thought, "Why do people do this? They couldn't possibly be getting anything out of it."

But, at this point, I knew that the yoga poses and postures were my only option for some kind of exercise and movement. I stepped into a beginner's class, and then I found myself taking another. It wasn't long before I discovered how much better I felt afterward. My heart rate stabilized, and I felt energetic for the first time I could remember.

Eventually, my thyroid problem resolved, but I continued to have regular dates with my yoga mat. I wanted to keep going and to understand why I felt so different when a yoga class was over than I had with any other workout.

The more I practiced, the better I did. After each class, I always wanted to keep going.

I soon realized that yoga was more than poses and alignment. Where I once laughed during yoga, I unexpectedly found it a safe place to work through my emotions. I could deal with stress, problems at work, and just clear my head. I could count on my yoga to revitalize me for whatever business task was at hand or disconnect from work after class because I didn't want to ruin the relaxation feeling I had afterward.

For me, yoga became my Balance. I discovered that my practice offered many solutions to my problems. It calmed my mind and increased my focus and concentration. It allowed me to be fully present at all times, letting go of my emotions and trusting myself to make the right decisions and not be influenced by inaction, or just remembering to pause and breathe.

I realized how challenging yoga could be—not only physically but also mentally. It takes courage to get on a yoga mat because you have to focus and not get distracted—by your body, your mind, how you move (and shouldn't move), and balance. If you lose your focus, it's possible for you to fall. This experience is such a wonderful parallel to my business life. If you are not mindful about all aspects, or get distracted, you will tumble and have to get back up again.

My yoga journey was invaluable during a difficult fork in the road of my life. Since then, I have continued to explore and grow beyond my individual practice. I have studied yoga philosophy and trained with top teachers. I became a certified yoga teacher, and well, my entrepreneur side overcame me again, and I now own a yoga studio.

Yoga has become my Balance of the B^3 Method, and it has helped me to be a better businesswoman. My work on my mat has given me new ways to deal with stress at work and in my personal life so that I can better deal with the experiences that we all deal with on a daily basis.

The first time I was finally able to touch my toes (after having a preconceived notion that touching my toes was out of reach), I was elated. I realized that my resistance was the stress that I hold internally and had never released. I just needed to not rush it, have patience, and with practice and time, it came.

That's such a great analogy for business every day. Yes, we can reach our potential, yes, we can overcome obstacles, yes we can deal with setbacks— yes, we can literally touch our toes—with the right practice and execution and patience along the way.

Keep in mind that if your Balance does not interest you, inspire you, and provide some excitement, you are not going to stick with it especially not for the long haul. It will become another place where you feel stress in your life.

Yoga is my primary Balance, but it may not be yours, so how do you discover *your* Balance? Sometimes you might stumble across it like I did, or find it through trial and error—try this activity and that activity until something sticks—but I have found that most people already know their Balance, they just don't admit it or recognize it.

Here's a question for you: What activity, hobby, or interest makes you happy? Don't think too hard about it, just react to the question. What springs to mind? Is it one thing or several? Write them down. Now ask yourself: "Why don't you do it on a regular basis?"

If you can't think of something, then go back to your childhood. So often our source of enjoyment is something we experienced and loved as a child but for whatever reason gave up.

Think back: What did you *really* enjoy doing when you were little? It could be anything—an organized sport, membership in a special club like Boy Scouts or Girls Scouts, or just spending time alone with your toys and games. What was it? Now ask yourself, "Why did you give it up?"

Odds are, you probably didn't realize it was as important to you at the time, or thought it was something mature adults don't waste their time with, or maybe your interest turned elsewhere.

That happened to me, too. Starting from when I was a child through my high school years, I played the viola and painted. I really enjoyed them both. It was not only fun, but also it was a creative outlet and provided some separation from the everyday stress of school—time just disappeared.

I eventually put my viola in the case and stored away my paints because I no longer had the time to practice when heading off to college and later becoming a CPA.

Years later, when I was deep in my career, I took a test called The Birkman Method with an executive coach. The test is a workplace psychological assessment developed by organizational psychologist Roger Birkman, PhD. The test's construction and analysis is meant to provide insight into what drives a person's behavior with the goal of creating greater choice and self-responsibility. It measures elements like social behaviors, needs or expectations, stress reactions, organizational strengths, occupational preferences, and personal interests.[5]

As I filled out the section on personal interests, it became quite clear to me what the results would be. The questions were designed to isolate what activities you find enjoyable. The point was to help steer you into a career that better complements you, or find out how your interests may translate into the business environment. In other words, when you are doing what feels natural to you, it doesn't feel like work.

Before I even looked at the results, I knew in my heart that art and music would be at the top. After all, that is what I knew came naturally to me. And sure enough they were.

Why wasn't this a surprise? Yes, I knew what those two interests meant to me, but I never saw them as either a path to a new career, or as another source of my Balance. I subconsciously pushed those passions down deep inside and ignored them because it was not my chosen career path or work experience.

Even though it seems obvious now, that test was another awakening. It helped me tap back into those childhood activities I loved so much that are completely different from my workday.

I grew up playing classical violin and viola but always dreamed of playing guitar. When my son was seven years old, the instrument he chose to play was electric guitar. It struck me then—it's not too late for me to learn guitar, and it would be fun to do this with my son. So I chose to learn the bass guitar.

The bass was a good fit: not only did it allow me to play with my son, but it also solved the void I had in my life that was exposed through the testing I had completed. I was now able to get back to my love of rock and learn to play music from bands like AC/DC, the Cult, Judas Priest, and Iron Maiden. I quickly found that playing music was a way to tap into my creative mind. This activity was completely opposite from what I did at work and provided a way for me to disconnect from my day and immerse myself in something I love.

When I'm on my bass, or just practicing certain notes or riffs, I can't be thinking about something else. I have to be fully engaged in my hand and finger movements, and listening to the changing chords. If not, everything else will sound like the buzz of an electric razor.

I have found that bass playing is also an excellent way to clear my head from a long, overwhelming day at work, and it challenges me to use different skills while improving my existing ones. Many times when I'm stuck with a work problem, I can pick up my bass for a few minutes, go through some riffs, and then come back to the business situation with a brand new perspective or a clearer mind.

So now, besides my yoga, I have learned the bass guitar and have enjoyed playing the rock music that I grew up with. I have gotten so involved in it that I have even started a pseudo family band with my husband and kids.

It's fun, it offers another way for us to all bond, and best of all for me, it provides another source for my Balance.

How Much Balance Do You Need?

How much time do you really need for true Balance? It can vary from person to person. There appears to be no ideal amount of me time that works for everyone, especially in how it relates to improving work-life harmony, overall happiness, and job satisfaction.

What does appear important, though, is to focus on quality—not quantity. It does not matter how much time you devote to your Balance as long as it is fulfilling.

Look at this 2015 study led by Almuth McDowall, PhD of Birkbeck College, University of London. They explored this concept to get a better idea of how much "me" time people need as well as how it equates to their work performance. They examined 344 professional workers, men and women. The researchers asked them to fill out a questionnaire about how they juggled the demands of work and home and their general satisfaction with their lives.

The amount of me time this group reported ranged from as little as three hours per week to as much as fifty hours!

The quality of this me time, no matter the duration, fell along these lines—40 percent described their me time as good and 42 percent as average.

Only 8 percent said their me time was very good, which was the highest available rating. However, those who rated their me time as very good enjoyed better work-life balance, overall well-being, and were more engaged at work. Just good or average was not good enough to have a powerful effect.[6]

This is only one study, but it reflects the approach you should have with your Balance. Choose something that really brings you pleasure and not more stress. Do not choose it because of convenience, ease, or "what everyone else does."

Once you have your Balance in place, then you can begin to apply the B³ Method components. The next chapters show you how the B³ Method can help with some of the most common issues in business that people face as they try to establish optimal work-life harmony:

1. How to be more present and productive (chapter 3)

2. How to find and maintain confidence and tame the ego (chapter 4)

3. How to build personal connections (chapter 5)

Odds are you have issues with one (or all of them), and if you don't, I guarantee you will at some point during your career. With the tools you learn from this book, you will be ready to tackle these issues when they arise.

B³ BASICS

Most people already know their Balance if they ask themselves the right questions. These questions can help you identify activities about which you are passionate and will help you brainstorm additional ideas for yourself:

- **Look outside reality.** What is your fantasy job (even if it's not realistic)?

- **Dream.** What is something you have dreamed about trying but talked yourself out of doing?

- **Look to your childhood for inspiration.** What did you enjoy doing as a child? It doesn't matter whether it was a team sport, arts and crafts, or board games. What activity was always fun for you and made you feel happy?

- **Try complementary activities.** If music is your thing, but playing an instrument is not, try attending concerts or collecting vintage records or even guitars as your outlet.

- **Use social media platforms.** For example, if food is your creative outlet, whether making or just trying different cuisines, begin an Instagram or Pinterest account that is just about food, or create a blog series about your interest and experiences.

- **Make a creativity board.** Fill a large poster or bulletin board with a collage of images, quotes, articles, and people that you find inspiring. As your board evolves, you will begin to note a pattern of what interests you.

B³ BRAINSTORMING

B³ BRAINSTORMING

_____

_____

_____

_____

_____

_____

_____

_____

_____

_____

_____

_____

_____

_____

_____

_____

_____

_____

_____

_____

3

BEING PRESENT

How being mindful can lead to being more productive

Years ago, I went to a colleague's brother's funeral to support him during his time of loss. I had never met his brother before, but after attending his funeral, his life made an impact on me from that day forward.

His friends and family had prepared personal reflections they were going to share during the funeral. They didn't share their comments with each other in advance.

One after the other, each person went to the front and gave a eulogy, and it was soon obvious the speeches had a common theme. All mentioned that they had been his best friend.

Eventually it became a humorous moment as everyone began his or her speech with, "I thought I was his best friend too!"

So, why did all of them think they were his best friend? It became apparent as more and more of them spoke that it was because he had always been completely present when he was with each person.

One person said, "He never wore a watch, but somehow he was never late and he was always on time to everything."

Another said, "When he was with you, he was completely focused on you and didn't get distracted."

As simple as it sounds, these statements are lessons for us all on how to live a life of intention. Most of us want to achieve this, but based on our busy lives and all the demands we have, it's hard to be mentally conscious of where we are every day.

The message behind these examples was really about being in the present moment all the time: being present with the people you love, the people you work with, and the people that surround you in your everyday life.

It's so easy to get distracted when we talk with someone on the phone or try to work surrounded by buzzing emails and texts or that polite knock-knock on the office door.

How often do we step back and take stock of how we make people feel? Instead, most of us are concerned more about how we feel individually and not enough about how we are affecting others.

Inherently, I believe most people want to be the nicest, most caring, well-intentioned people. However, if we aren't giving the people we are with the undivided attention they deserve, their personal feeling may be that what they had to say or offer was not worthy of our full consideration. I don't think most of us mean to do this, including myself; there is just too much "noise" in the world that distracts us and keeps us from being fully engaged.

Think for a moment how different our lives would be if we were completely focused without distraction on each thing we did? How different would people feel about each other if we were all completely present and focused on the person with whom we were spending time? If we step back and learn from observing how people feel, it may cause us to allot the right amount of time to everyone.

Instinctively, we could recognize when we have reached the end of one experience and know when it is time to move on to the next one without an appointment reminder. If we took this into our workday rather than trying to multitask, could we produce more and would our decisions be better? Maybe we would start limiting the number of things we do, so that we aren't distracted and feeling the need to multitask, and instead, we could be fully present in each moment.

BUSINESS

Coping with office distractions, multitasking, and technology

Sadly, businesses are set up to distract. The workplace is constant activity, stimulus, and energy. There are times when we feed off that, and it actually helps us be more mentally engaged, but often business sets up constant roadblocks to our attention.

Workplace distractions can be like land mines, hidden everywhere in your daily path, but you have no idea when you might run into one. Some distractions are obvious and ongoing like email, social media, phone calls, texts, meetings, and the coworker who wants to pop in and chat about his or her weekend.

Other distractions, however, are subtler and hidden in plain sight. For instance, research from Cornell University found that low-level noise in open-office plans can increase worker stress and decrease their motivation.[7]

But perhaps the biggest distraction in business is our desire to multi-task. As I mentioned earlier, the boom of technology has allowed us to do more at any given time. After all, our generation is the multitasking generation: Typing, texting, calling, instant messaging—we can do it all at one time. Or think we can.

However, our brains are not wired to multitask. Julie Morgenstern, author of *Time Management from the Inside Out,* explained in an interview with *Forbes* that the brain is not designed to efficiently switch between tasks. In fact, she says "it takes four times longer to recognize new things" when you bounce back and forth. You may believe you are doing more by juggling several things at once, but it takes more of your time, not less.[8]

Your intelligence can also take a hit with multitasking. An often-cited study by researchers from the University of London found that people who multitasked during cognitive tasks had a temporary drop in IQ scores. Men in the study experienced a fifteen-point drop while women had a five-point decline.[9] The researchers added that the mental effect was like staying up all night.

No matter the source, though, the final result is that distractions negatively impact productivity and eventually a business' bottom line.

Gloria Mark, PhD, is a professor who studies digital distraction at the University of California, Irvine. Her research has shown that *any* interruption, no matter the source or duration, changes how you work.[10]

She also has found that there's typically, on average, only about three minutes of consistent focus before an employee gets interrupted—either by digital means (email, texts, phone calls, etc.), personal interruptions, or even when you interrupt yourself with a wandering mind. Once you are distracted, it can take time before you refocus again. In fact, Dr. Mark says it can be as long as *twenty-three minutes* before you get back to the work you were doing before the interruption occurred.[11]

From a business perspective, those lost minutes add up to significant lost productivity and thus revenue. A 2011 survey conducted by the software company harmon.ie and research firm uSamp estimated that businesses might lose more than $10 million a year—or more than $10,000 per employee—thanks in part to regular workplace distractions.[12] Yikes!

Don't get me wrong. The advances in technology over the past two decades have transformed how we live and work. Take our improved ability to communicate, for example. You can talk to anyone, anywhere, at almost any time. You can do it with video, conference calls, FaceTime, email, text messages, you name it, from a laptop, tablet, or smartphone. This has really expanded how, when, and with whom we do business. More work can be done quicker and more efficiently.

As a global executive, I work with people in the UK, US, Australia, and New Zealand. Everyone works in different time zones. Technology has allowed me to create and sustain these working relationships as if we are in the same country or time zone. Twenty years ago this would not have been possible.

Perhaps technology's strongest asset is the ability to enhance work speed and efficiency, but at what price? Technology allows us to do more work, which we brazenly embrace.

Why do we work so much? Because we can. When our parents left their jobs at the end of the day, there was really no way for them to bring it home, their only alternative was to stay at the office later or come in earlier. But we have access to work 24/7, which creates this ongoing temptation to always be on the job. Who hasn't flipped open the laptop or checked their mobile phone in bed at 10 p.m.? Or scrolled through their email while watching TV?

Then there is the ease at which meetings can be arranged. In the past, meetings were rare, big-time events that you could easily plan your workday or even workweek around. Now, with the evolution of meeting applications and video conferencing, people can be pulled into meetings at a moment's notice. As we have all experienced at one time, meetings can become vacuums of wasted time, especially when there is little discipline involved in how and why they are organized.

It is no surprise then that America is the most overworked country in the world. A 2014 Gallup poll found that adults who are employed full-time work an average of forty-seven hours per week—almost a full workday longer than the standard five-day, eight-hour work schedule. In fact, almost 40 percent of these workers said they typically work at least fifty hours per week.[13]

And more doesn't always mean better.

Besides the health issues related to burned out, stressed out workers, putting in extra time like this doesn't even pay off in terms of work performance—at least in the long term.

Information, compiled by the company Business Roundtable, found that employees can produce more when they stick to a heavy workload of sixty to seventy hours, like when trying to hit a tight deadline. Yet, the effect lasts only a few weeks. However, increasing the number of working hours from the usual forty hours to sixty hours does not result in more productivity.[14]

The reason? Most people do their best work when they work between two and six hours, according to the research. Their best work tends to be behind them after an eight-hour day. By hour nine, their production begins to drop.

Don't be fooled into thinking those extra hours get you extra points from your boss. One study led by Erin Reid, a professor at Boston University's Questrom School of Business, found that supervisors could not tell which employees worked eighty hours and which ones only pretended to work that much.[15]

And then there is the guilt factor.

Research reported in the *Harvard Business Review* concluded that a typical frontline supervisor or midlevel manager only has 6.5 hours, on average, per full-time workweek to get their own work done after you subtract time devoted to meetings and processing e-communication, and other time-wasting office activities.[16]

And what happens next? People are forced (or more likely think they have to) work extra hours to make up for this lost time, the so-called guilt factor.

I can definitely relate to that.

Early in my career, I worked for a company in South Florida. My job there was to create a financial plan for logistics contracts on which we were bidding. My understanding of operational business process efficiency was key so we could be profitable on those contracts. Around this time, I became pregnant with my first child. My initial thought, as it related to my career, was that it wasn't going to change anything. I personally thought that I could still keep up with everything and drive my career forward.

However, I was instructed by my doctor to be on bed rest at twenty-six weeks. No problem, I thought. With my computer and phone, I could easily set up a temporary office in my bed.

I negotiated my new work schedule and thought everything would stay the same in terms of my workweek. But I soon found the line between my work and my home life was blurred.

Pretty quickly, I got into a pattern where I worked around the clock dealing with clients in different time zones. I took my phone to my regular exams so I would never miss a call. In fact, as embarrassing as it is to admit, I would ask my husband Rob to hold my phone to take any incoming calls in case anyone wanted me while I met with my doctor. I was afraid that I would miss something.

Many of us have this mindset. If we can work, we think we should, because there is so much work to do. However, we must not give in to the convenience and temptation of technology and, instead, learn how to balance the demands and pressure so that we don't work twenty-four hours a day.

Working remotely does not prevent you from the temptations to over-work. I have seen this firsthand. My husband Rob works from home, and despite the flexibility this arrangement offers, he eventually found himself working more and at different hours, weekend days, and partial holidays.

His lunch hour was grabbing something from the kitchen and marching back to his office. Even his "me" time turned into no time. Rob says, "many times in the morning I had planned to work out in my home gym—to create Balance for myself—but I would find instead, I was going into my office first to log in and do a quick check of email. That then led to me sitting down for just a minute to respond to those 'quick' and 'easy' emails.

The next thing I realized was that twenty to thirty minutes would pass, and then I had less time to work out. By then, my mind had partially drifted into work mode, so I would lose my workout motivation."

BALANCE AND BLISS

Your goal to be more present and mindful, and thus improve productivity in Business, means learning to avoid the daily onslaught of distractions so you are not vulnerable to distractions when they occur. You can accomplish this by focusing on three main areas: time management, mindfulness, and inspiration.

TIME MANAGEMENT

When we are not organized with our time, it is easier to get distracted. We are not focused, our minds wander, and before we know it hours (or the entire day) may have passed without accomplishing anything of importance. That wasted time adds up too. Check out these startling stats from a 2014 survey of 750 employees connected by Salary.com[17]:

- 89 percent said they waste at least some time at work daily.

- 31 percent waste about thirty minutes daily.

- 31 percent waste about an hour per day.

- 16 percent waste about two hours daily.

What are the main causes for this wasted time? Another survey, conducted by Harris Poll for CareerBuilder, queried more than 3,000 workers across various industries and found—probably to no big surprise—that talking on the cell phone and texting was the number-one time waster, followed by gossiping, being on the Internet or social media, being distracted by coworkers, attending meetings, and responding to email.[18]

Now, some of these behaviors are necessary for work—you have to communicate with people, respond to emails, and be in meetings—but when they creep into your daily workday, they can become the ultimate time-suckers.

Managing your daily work may feel like a job, but it doesn't have to be. You don't need to radically change how you approach your work, but you should adopt certain behaviors that can keep you on track—and distractions to a minimum. Here are some Balance strategies you can try to see if they work for you to improve your time management and cut down on distractions.

BALANCE: Plan every day. Without a daily schedule, it is easy to get distracted by unknown events. If you are more aware of what you want to accomplish and keep it handy, you have a constant reminder that your attention is needed elsewhere. Some people keep a simple to-do list, email their task list to themselves, use apps to organize their to-do list, or keep an audio recording. Choose something that works best for you and that you can utilize daily, and most important, keep it with you at all times.

BLISS

- **Use your calendar.** There are many kinds of online scheduling apps available that you can download on your computer, tablet, or smartphone. These can help you stay committed to daily planning since you spend so much time with electronic devices. They also can alert you when it's time to move to another task, or you can schedule reminders that a certain activity needs to begin.

BALANCE: Identify where you waste the most time. If you find your daily planning too daunting and it has the effect of becoming a distraction, take a step back and look at how you spend your time during the day, and what times of day you have more or less energy. This may help you prioritize which jobs you need to focus on early in the day and which ones can be saved for later. This will also keep you from overextending yourself by thinking you can cross off a long list every day.

BLISS

- An online tool like RescueTime.com can track your time spent on applications and websites, emails, and social media. With this information in hand, you can better prioritize your day and identify how you spend most of your time—and where you waste it. It can also identify what times of day you are most active in all these areas, so that you can better plan for your energy levels, like when you complete daily office tasks versus having meetings.

BALANCE: Divide your day into two halves. Your energy and discipline are often highest in the morning, so reserve that time for larger tasks that require more mental effort. For example, block your calendar to get your own work done in the morning and schedule conference calls and meetings in the afternoon.

BLISS

- **Always take your lunch break.** Lunchtime has become a lost tradition. We eat more often at our desk because we think we don't have the time. But you need that brief time off whether it is a full hour or just thirty minutes. Your lunchtime can be how you divide your day in half. But you have to take it in order to reenergize.

- **Work in ninety-minute segments.** Florida State University researchers studied elite performers, like athletes, actors, musicians, and even chess players, and found that their best performances occurred in sessions that lasted no more than ninety minutes.[19]

Forget the nose-to-grindstone approach. After ninety minutes of uninterrupted work or meetings, step away and take a break.

- **Take a five-minute break.** When you ping-pong between meetings, give yourself a break before going straight from one meeting to the next. I like to always set aside five minutes between meetings to just recenter my mind, calm my body, and redirect my attention to the moment. That way I can be fully present and engaged for the next encounter rather than having my mind lingering in the past.

BALANCE: Set up temporary electronic walls. I know this one is tough. We are so plugged in—so how can we essentially pull the plug? It can be scary, yet quite liberating for the mind. Turn off your phone and put it out of sight when meeting with someone else. Close your web browser, emails, and notifications so you can't check social media or other distracting websites. It can feel daunting at first, so begin small and try it for short durations like fifteen to twenty minutes. I used this approach, and it helped me ease into cutting myself off from the world. I realized it's fine not to be accessible to everyone and everything all the time.

BLISS

- **Block website usage.** Google offers extensions called StayFocus and Block Site that can block chosen Chrome websites for specific periods of time.

- **Hang up the "do not disturb" sign.** Whether you work on-site or off-site, you have to be mindful of the "ambush" meetings when coworkers pop their heads into your office or IM you to chat. Turn your phone or computer status to "away," "busy," or "do not disturb"; or close your office door; or hang a sign in front of your work area whenever you cannot afford to lose your focus or time.

My husband, Rob, uses this approach with great success because he works off-site and people can't see whether he is available to talk. "I also do this when I take my personal breaks to ensure that I get my needed time away without interruptions," he says.

MINDFULNESS

What does it mean to be fully present or mindful? In its classic definition, mindfulness is a mental state of active, open attention on the present. You are not focused on the past or the future but the present, right here, right now, with whatever you are doing. It is hard to measure—but you know it when you feel it.

Mindfulness probably conjures the image of a calm yogi meditating with crossed legs, eyes closed, in silence, oblivious of everything around him or her.

But in business, mindfulness might represent something else—those precious periods when you are fully focused and engaged in what is in front of you at any moment—completing a task, listening to a conversation, participating in a meeting, reading a memo. Your mind and attention is not wandering or collecting random thoughts like what you will have for lunch or what you will do after work, or getting distracted by texts or emails. Instead all your energy and brainpower is streamlined like a laser beam on only one thing at a time and nothing else.

We have all had these moments, and they are wonderful. It's like feeling a runner's high or operating in what athletes call "the zone." You get stuff done, you feel energized, and you feel you can accomplish anything.

But the problem is that we often believe this should be our natural state all the time. We then become frustrated when we are distracted and lose our focus even for an instance.

To be mindful, your thinking needs to change. It is not about being present all the time, no matter what, but rather about being able to turn on that laser beam of attention when it's needed and not being so easily distracted that the beam gets shut off at inappropriate times. Here are some ideas that might help.

BALANCE: Practice active listening. Great team leaders are engaged in their team members. They understand what they need, their strengths, weaknesses, and challenges. They know this because they connect mentally and emotionally with each team member. Team leaders listen to what their team members have to say and respond appropriately.

Think about your personal relationships. When your partner listens to what you say, and is engaged in a conversion, he or she has a clearer understanding of what you need and what you want to achieve. In return, you are more receptive (and appreciative) to what he or she says and to any advice or insight that's given.

The same approach applies here. When team leaders better understand their team members' needs, they can offer the right support, guidance, motivation, and feedback to help the entire team succeed. And team members will notice this and respond equally. They will be more motivated to go the extra mile for you and the team. Those are the kind of people you want. When you are setting the example of practicing mindfulness, it permeates throughout your team.

One way you can do this is to practice active listening. We have all had those moments in meetings when our mind wanders and we can't keep track of what people say; or when we are engaged in a conversation but can't stay focused on the individual.

Remember the story of the man's funeral? Perhaps the most essential quality everyone praised about him was how engaged he was with everyone he met.

If you can train your brain to be 100 percent engaged with everyone with whom you converse—with a larger group, an individual, whether in person, or on the phone—it can help you stay focused during your work and block distractions when they arise.

BLISS

- **Maintain eye contact.** When you are not visually focused on people as they speak, your mind can easily wander because you don't have a central point to keep you grounded. Put aside anything that might make you lose your gaze: paper, pens, phone, reading materials. Look at the person and stay connected while they are speaking and presenting information to you. When you see someone speak you are much more likely to focus on what he or she is saying. That means, as hard as it is, don't leave your phone on the table, put it away and check it after your meeting.

- **Don't be a sentence grabber.** Let people finish their thoughts or points before adding your comments. You can even reiterate what they said before adding your own comments, such as "What I heard you say was . . . My perspective is . . ." If you are focused on what you want to say, you won't be listening to what others are saying.

- **Use brief, but positive, phrases to maintain the conversation.** For example, "Oh?" "Then?" "And?" and "I understand." These trigger words can also keep your mind engaged because you have to respond to what has been said.

- **Probe**. Ask questions to draw people out and get deeper and more meaningful information. For example, "What do you think would happen if you . . . ?" Asking questions offers new information that can stimulate your thinking and thus your listening. Also, ensure you understand what they are trying to get across by restating it, "What I heard you say was . . . , is that correct?"

BALANCE: Practice meditation. Meditation can mean many things to different people. I like to think of meditation as brief periods where you can calm your mind from the surrounding chaos and slow everything down to engage your mind. It often doesn't take a lot of time or even effort to center yourself and be more aware.

Meditation can focus on a single point like counting your breaths, visualizing a certain image, or just picturing a calming, singular action. For example, yoga—my Balance—has offered me a form of meditation by teaching me how to block out my surroundings and focus on my breath. When I am on the mat and moving into a pose—or even a challenging one like an arm balance (lifting your body off the ground is never easy)—I must be mindful about each movement, stay focused, and not be hard on myself if the pose is not perfect that day. Without removing mental distractions, I may unintentionally fall out of the pose.

BLISS

- **Give your brain a power nap.** If you anticipate getting mentally stuck, maybe before a meeting you're dreading, or a conversation you'd rather not have, give your brain a quick splash of cold water. If I'm mentally dragging before I head into my next meeting, whether with my team or a client, in person or on the phone, I take two minutes to close my eyes, calm my breathing, shut everything down, and just be still It's like a power nap for the brain and allows me to reset.

- **Focus on your emotions.** Here is a simple meditation exercise that focuses on managing your emotions from Richard Miller, PhD, founding president of the Integrative Restoration Institute.[20]

    1. Sit in a comfortable position and close your eyes. Note and welcome the sounds and sensations around you—the air on your skin, the sound of your breathing. Note the emotion you are feeling. Don't judge it or try to change it. Just acknowledge it.

2. Next, think of an opposite emotion or a memory that invites the opposite reaction. If you are stressed, maybe you can recall a vacation when you felt nothing but serenity.

3. Move on to the next emotion and repeat the exercise. Sense how your body and mind change when you focus on the opposite emotion.

4. Do this several times and then open your eyes when ready.

INSPIRATION

Your work environment, either at the office or home, is a source of inspiration. If you feel empowered and inspired by your surroundings, you will be more productive and won't be as tempted by distractions.

There may be limits to what you can change in your work space, but make every effort to create something that you find stimulating, whether it is pictures, inspirational messages within easy eyesight, music, candles, furniture, plants, artwork, etc. Make it a reflection of your interests and personality and needs.

BALANCE: Take mental breaks. Even with your best intentions, there will be times when distractions take over, and you will have moments where your mind wanders and no matter how hard you try, you can't seem to stay focused. It happens. So, don't be discouraged when this occurs. Just recognize it, acknowledge it, and make small changes to refocus your attention.

BLISS

- **Step away from the pinball machine.** When you have one meeting after another, or are jumping from one task to the next, like a pinball machine, take a moment for a brief rest period before diving into the next endeavor. Even if you only have ten minutes, take a walk, sit quietly in your office with the door closed, play some music, or read some articles. It can even be as simple as taking several deep breaths. It's truly amazing how we forget to breathe throughout the day. The point is to give yourself a mini timeout where you and your brain can take a step back to recharge. This way you will be fully engaged for the next item on the to-do list without carrying the distracting baggage along from the previous item.

- **Create your mantra.** If there are inspirational quotes or actions you want to be reminded of, you can post signs with the quotes so your eye will catch them during the day to remind you to reset. I have sticky notes on my computer as reminders, so that when I see them, I adjust my thoughts and respond differently. There are apps and websites you can go to for daily inspirations. One of my favorites is www.dailyom.com.

- **Take a Balance break.** Jenna McHugh, vice president at a Fortune 500 company, uses running as her Balance. She competes in marathons and has qualified eight times for the Boston Marathon in the past three years. She turns to her Balance as a way to tap into inspiration and often laces up her shoes for a run as a work break. "Running produces the best ideas for me," says Jenna. "Many times before I head out for a run, I come up with a 'thinking challenge'— a question I want to answer or a problem I want to solve. I have come up with ideas for my daughter's birthday party, a list of topics to discuss with our CFO in our next meeting, and ideas to help market our company's 401(k) match. Running is like a meeting with myself." You can do this too. Keep part of your Balance around you for times when you need to regroup your attention. Play the guitar? Have an extra instrument in the corner that you can strum. Drawing? Pull out your sketchpad.

BALANCE: Get some (natural) light. One part of your environment that can have a far-reaching effect on inspiration is your surrounding light. Your brain reacts positively in well-lit environments. A 2014 study published in the *Journal of Clinical Sleep Medicine* found that employees with windows in the workplace received 173 percent more white light exposure during work hours and slept an average of forty-six minutes more per night than employees who did not have the natural light exposure in the workplace.[21] There was also a trend for workers in offices with windows to have more physical activity than people without windows.

BLISS

- **Get close to the window.** Try to place your work space as close to windows as possible (within at least twenty-five feet). Not an option? Go outside during the day for brief exposure to sunshine.

- **Use blue light.** Harvard researchers explored how blue light—also known as short wavelength light—affects alertness and performance in a daytime work setting. They found that during a six-and-a-half-hour workday, the workers exposed to blue light had fewer attention lapses and faster reaction times when they did performance tests compared with those workers who were exposed to regular light.[22]

B³ BASICS

How to avoid distractions and return to the moment when your mind wanders:

- **Practice active listening.** Look at people when they speak, ask questions when appropriate, and don't interrupt.

- **Wake up with a focus—not your emails.** Refrain from looking at anything for the first hour when you wake up (it can wait) and use that time to engage your mind with thinking, reading, planning, reflecting.

- **Give yourself daily breaks from all electronics.** Disconnect for an hour every day. Turn off your phone, walk away from your computer. It will be hard at first, but your mind will come to welcome those brief respites.

- **Plan your workday for today and tomorrow.** Schedule big tasks that require the most attention and focus early in the day, if possible, when energy levels are the highest.

- **Take a two-minute break** when you are mentally dragging before your next interaction. Set a timer on your phone so you aren't checking it while you take the break. Allow yourself at least two minutes to calm your mind, let go, and regroup. You will be amazed at how quickly this can refresh you.

- **Stay nourished.** As simple as it is, drink water throughout the day. It will revive your energy in a healthy way, without caffeine.

- **Hang up the "do not disturb" sign.** Turn your IM status to "away" or "busy." Take advantage of these tools whenever you cannot afford to lose your focus or time.

The recipe for a successful business often contains three main ingredients:

1. A great idea

2. A great plan

3. A great work ethic and a passion for the business

B³ BRAINSTORMING

B³ BRAINSTORMING

4

BUILDING CONFIDENCE

How to find and express
your hidden voice

Yes, there are other variables that come into play—like start-up capital, competition, economic environment, and a bit of luck, but if you narrow down success to its key components, odds are these three would stand out.

Yet there is something else that binds all three together: Confidence. You must believe in your idea, have trust in your plan of execution, and have faith that your hard work and perseverance will pay off. It is impossible to achieve anything without an underlying foundation of confidence.

If you work in a business, rather than owning it, confidence, or a lack of it, can be what keeps you stuck in your current position or propels you forward on the fast track.

When I launched my accounting business at age twenty-seven, I didn't have any connections or really know how to go about finding customers. I began to advertise and throw my name out there to see what would work, but I quickly realized I had to network.

I visited industry organizations and business gatherings; shook hands; told my story; talked about my business and what I do; handed out business cards; and scheduled breakfast, lunch, and dinner to network, in addition to sending out mailers to local businesses and cold calling. During this time, I didn't have one client, and my business was nothing more than the name. In essence, I had to have the confidence to market myself and the belief that future clients would benefit from what I was offering.

When I met people, I always made sure to project confidence and passion for what I do. I put myself out there with no guarantee that anything would happen. Were there really hard days when I thought it would never work? Sure. But soon enough, my efforts paid off, and the calls from clients began to come in.

We know when we feel confident and when we don't. We can easily recognize confidence in others: healthy posture, clear commanding voice, strong eye contact, and powerful body language. We look at some people and immediately recognize it.

For most people, the challenge with confidence is simple—we are not sure how to get it and, then, how to retain it.

We discuss how to become more confident later in this chapter, but first let's look at another issue. Is there a way to turn your confidence on when it's needed, keep it going so it can last longer, and have it occur more often in the future?

It turns out you can. First, you have to see what confidence looks like in the brain.

Researchers have begun to explore how self-confidence may be sustained. One way is through a process called "decoded neurofeedback," which involves identifying complex patterns of brain activity and then giving feedback based on that brain activity. Here is how it works.

In one 2016 study, published in the journal *Nature Communications*, a UCLA research team had subjects sit in an fMRI scanner, which monitored their brain activity while they were given a simple perceptual task to perform. Every time their brain pattern appeared to show high activity in the front of the brain—called the ventromedial prefrontal cortex (a sign of confidence)—the subjects received a monetary reward. When they showed low confidence, they received less money.

When they repeated the tests, the researchers found that those who received rewards for high confidence were more confident in their ability. They saw the benefit of confidence (in this case a reward) and were more confident the next time even though their result was unknown to them.[23]

It is only one study, but the findings suggest that you may be able to program yourself to be more confident. You can do this by ensuring you recognize your accomplishments—so when a similar situation arises, you can tap into your confidence knowing you have had success before. Being good at recognizing the positive work you do and giving yourself praise, rather than internal defeating talk, is important for maintaining confidence. Next time, notice the internal talk and flip the dialogue to what you have accomplished rather than what didn't work. It's a lifelong exercise to take control of your thoughts rather than letting them control you.

Insecurity. Self-doubt. Lack of confidence. It goes by many names and affects people in different ways, but the result is often the same: we can lack the ability to pursue our full capability without having confidence in ourselves. Things such as being afraid of failure, ridicule, or criticism can cause our fears. However, confidence can either lift you to success or become a barrier that keeps you down.

Every businessperson wants more confidence. Look at all the great modern day business icons from Bill Gates to Sheryl Sandberg. They know what they want to achieve and do it. They exude confidence and never question their ability or choices.

This is not always true. All successful people will tell you stories about when they faced crippling self-doubt and wondered if they would ever make it. But instead of giving up, they pushed through failures and downtimes and stayed positive that their efforts would pay off.

A colleague of mine, Misty Megia, is the vice president of a learning company. A dancer since age five, she continues to be involved in the arts, either as a performer or choreographer/director. It is her Balance. She participates in up to two shows a year, while balancing her business career. Planning for a show can take from four to six weeks. Rehearsals are often three hours per night during the week and another twelve hours on the weekend, either in dance studios or in renovated commercial spaces.

The confidence Misty has gained with her theatre work, and her ability to oversee all aspects of production, has prepared her for those moments when things do not go as planned. She likes to tell this story.

Once, she was speaking in Guatemala for a hardware company. Misty was not fluent in Spanish so she had a translator. She met with the company about an hour before the presentation to translate the language being used in order to get familiar with the overall presentation and the terminology she was going to use.

Her translator was late and didn't show up until about a half hour before the presentation. The audience was packed full of press and attendees from the technology conference. As Misty was reviewing the presentation with the translator with little time to go, she kept shaking her head from side to side. "Is everything okay?" The translator asked. Misty said it wasn't okay and quickly realized that she didn't understand many of the terms being used in the presentation.

"I was just about to go onstage before an audience I couldn't communicate with. Internal panic ensued. However, theater teaches you to search for a solution and never to panic on the outside," she says.

She and the translator took the stage. They asked the audience members whether they could help translate any of the words. For each term, someone raised his or her hand to volunteer to translate. Misty ended up doing her presentation by pointing around the audience like a disco dancer. The result—the presentation concluded with loud applause.

"Having that sense of how to fix something on the spot is definitely a theatre trait," she says. "You can't stop the show for a mistake—it must go on. I've had to tap dance in a show while the screw that was holding my taps together poked through the sole of my shoe and was digging into my foot. You figure out a way to do something differently. You look at what you need to do and adjust. You don't stop moving forward or give up—you figure out a solution that will work."

Of course, some people are more naturally confident than others. We have all met people who walk into a room and you can just feel the radiant confidence they exude. They stand tall, speak forcefully, and appear 100 percent certain of their abilities.

What about the rest of us? How can we be like that?

While both men and women battle confidence issues, I have found that women struggle with it differently—at least outwardly. A lot of it has to do with self-worth—women often do not value their abilities, even when they have clearly demonstrated their potential.

A 2011 study in the *American Sociological Review* surveyed 288 students who entered engineering programs at MIT, the University of Massachusetts at Amherst, the Franklin W. Olin College of Engineering, and Smith College. The study found that the women students took the same classes, took the same tests, and earned the same or higher grades as the male students. However, the women did not think a career in engineering was right for them and felt less confident in their ability to enter and succeed in the field.[24]

Why the gloomy talk? The researchers found the women's lack of confidence tended to focus on their personal reflection that they were only good at the social aspects of engineering—like teamwork and communications—and not the technical aspects. This was despite the fact that they demonstrated the necessary math and science skills in the classroom. In other words, they didn't think they could do it, so they didn't even bother to pursue an engineering career.

It's an all-too-familiar scenario. I see women stop themselves from applying for a better job because they think they are not ready or they are worried they might not succeed. I have seen women entrepreneurs not apply for the funding they need because they are afraid of possible rejection.

But here's the truth: You are never 100 percent ready for the next step. When an opportunity arises, you take it even when it is out of your comfort zone. The worst thing to happen is that you don't get the thing you applied for, but what you do gain is the knowledge of the application process and the ability to identify the gaps you do have, so that you fill those the next time. And there will be a next time.

Besides lost opportunities, a lack of confidence can hold you back because it can make you invisible. If you don't share your ideas, make suggestions for improvement, show others what you are capable of, it makes it harder to move forward. It may cause you to blend into the background and away from the action. People remember people who make an impact—whether with their voice or actions. Depending on your personality, there is always a way to contribute and show your value, if you are willing to put yourself out there.

Of course, men have their confidence issues too, but they are more likely to hide it. They have more pressure to succeed and advance because they are in constant competition with other males (and themselves).

Many people have the added burden of filling the perceived role of family provider as well. Much of their ultimate success rides on how well they present themselves to others. If men show even the slightest hint of low confidence, it can enforce an image that is hard to shake. They will be seen as a person not up for the task, not a team player, or lacking the necessary skills (even when they do possess them). It may give the impression to others that they lack the confidence to do an important job.

There is a lot of "be more confident" advice out there. It does not all work for everyone, but here are eight strategies to confront to overcome some of the main barriers that can keep you from being confident. They include:

1. Fearing failure

2. Overthinking

3. Thinking you can do everything

4. Thinking you *can't* do anything

5. Not knowing your purpose

6. Having trouble standing out

7. Underestimating your expertise

8. Lacking support

BUSINESS

Fearing failure

You may fail more times than you succeed in business. For every success story, there are hundreds of tales of previous failures. Trying and failing and trying again is part of the process. You must accept that you will not do everything right and you will make mistakes. Yes, some mistakes might have severe consequences, others might cause setbacks, but remember, no one started with nothing and reached the top without stumbles and tumbles along the way. No one.

You learn by failing. Thomas Edison made 1,000 unsuccessful attempts at inventing the light bulb. Jack London, author of the classic *Call of the Wild*, received more than 600 rejections before he sold his first story. Henry Ford went broke five times.

Mistakes are the path to success. In my own career, I have made a lot of mistakes, but most I do not regret. If those mistakes hadn't happened, I wouldn't have learned a better way or had the experience that I needed for my next opportunity.

If you really want something, do not let fear get in your way. Do not focus on all your reasons for not doing it. To succeed, you have to push through that fear and uncertainty no matter how intimidating or how rough the path may appear. Stop being afraid of what could go wrong and get excited about what could go right. Do that and you immediately gain more confidence.

BALANCE: Do something that invites failure. I know what you are thinking, "What? Why would I want to fail?" This is not about punishing yourself but rather teaching yourself how to become more comfortable with failing—and more important—learning what comes next. You need to accept failure (not run away from it) and gain wisdom from the experience.

That is what Greg Kyte, a CPA by trade, discovered through his Balance of stand-up comedy. Can you think of a more open invitation to failure than comedy? Here is what he did and why it was a boost to his confidence.

During his career as an accountant, Greg often battled anxiety especially when trying to navigate through new unfamiliar accounting software. It got so bad that his doctor prescribed Klonopin to help manage his episodes. However, the medication left him sleepy, which made him worry even more about not being able to do his job, and thus, only exaggerated his anxiety.

He turned to stand-up comedy to satisfy a childhood desire but also to combat his anxious behavior and gain greater confidence at work.

"There is a saying that tragedy plus time equals comedy. So when you do comedy, any tragedy or failure—although it sucks at the time—can lead to comedy," he says.

"Stand-up gives me courage to take bigger risks than I would otherwise. A lot of times when I approach a challenging or risky opportunity, and the potential for failure seems high, I tell myself—'The worst that can happen is I'll end up with a great story.'

"And it's absolutely true. Every time I choose to play it safe, I regret it. When I instead choose to throw myself into a risky opportunity, I either succeed, which is obviously great, or I get a fantastic story of dismal failure. And people LOVE to hear about dismal failure.

"In a way, stand-up comedy eliminates risk for me because if I take a big risk and win, I win big. And if I lose, I still kind of win. When you can't lose like that, you've got confidence."

You can do the same: Find something that you were always sure you would fail at the first time. And do it. The confidence to fail spurs the confidence to succeed. You may be amazed at how strong you will become from going through the experience and realize that you survived to do it again and, also, learned from the process.

BLISS

- **Do something with no goal in mind.** Try something with no objective. For instance, decide to interview for a job that you may have self-doubt or self-defeating thoughts about. The worst thing that can happen is that you don't get the job. But, even if you do not get the job, the opportunity to interview is good practice, and you will get feedback about where your gaps are. Taking the feedback and getting the experience you need will help you in your future success when you put yourself out there.

- **Use your Balance.** A new type of Balance is a wonderful way to do this. Your Balance is not about keeping score on how well you do or trying to reach a particular level of expertise—you will get better at most things the more you do them. The first time you do something, you may feel a touch of anxiety because you are not an expert. It is hard for us as adults to be a beginner and make mistakes. But as you become more comfortable, your confidence will naturally grow as you recognize your abilities. Your initial failure will be a path to success. For instance, with my Balance of playing bass guitar, I am still a novice. I repeatedly hit the wrong notes, lose my place, and have to start over. That is fine with me. I learn from my mistake and work to nail it the next time. When you get stuck, rather than giving up, stick with it. Go back to your Balance and use the lessons you have learned from your activities to deal with failure successfully.

BUSINESS

Overthinking

Have you ever obsessed over how to approach something only to end up so confused that you ultimately did nothing? You want to make carefully thought-out and calculated decisions, but there are times in business and in life when ignorance is bliss. The less you know or think about a situation and just go with your instinct without overthinking it, the better off you will be.

BALANCE: Focus on one task at a time. I do not let myself get overwhelmed with all the demands in my life or the possible ramifications of each decision I make (or don't make). I stay focused on each individual task at the moment: consulting with a customer, finishing a project, or speaking to a group of accountants or small business owners. If you focus on everything that is on your plate, at every moment, you will become overwhelmed.

BLISS

- **Look at the big picture.** I do not allow myself to succumb to thinking I will fail—instead, I set a vision in my head of what success looks like and stay focused on the big picture. I do my research, I put a plan together, and I execute it. If my plan does not work out as desired, I make corrections for the next time. If it fails entirely,

I note my mistakes and move on to the next opportunity. The most important part of a plan is that it remains agile. I can be flexible where I need to be or abandon what is not working. You want to be able to have that flexibility as you acquire more information to achieve your short-term and long-term vision. If I did not do this and let doubt and uncertainty creep in, it would chip away at my confidence.

- **Break it down.** The next time you feel your confidence waning when you are faced with a seemingly big task, try breaking it down into small parts and just focus on one thing at a time. For instance, when I'm giving a speech, I break it up into segments, like research, writing, and practicing. I don't look at the end result—speaking onstage under a spotlight in front of several hundred people. When it comes time for my speech, all the work and preparation is finished and all that is left is the execution.

BUSINESS

Thinking you can do everything

Sometimes a lack of confidence stems not from your ability but from your inability to do everything. Depending on your position and your needs, forming a supportive staff where you can outsource certain tasks and responsibilities can help offset the skills at which you are weak. This also helps you carve out the time you need for the higher-level work without being buried in details and burning yourself out.

BALANCE: Enlist a support staff. When I have done this—either in my accounting or yoga business—I always thought the people to whom I assign the work are better set up to dig into the details because that is their role.

It helps me to be more secure in decision making and confident in meeting deadlines.

BLISS

- **Assess yourself.** Make a list of what you are good at and where you think you fall short. If you need help, ask a trusted colleague, friend, or former employee. It may be hard to hear, but the information will be invaluable. You can then focus on how to capitalize on your strengths and get comfortable addressing the areas where you need to improve—and where you need help—which will only help grow your confidence.

BUSINESS

Thinking you *can't* do anything

Ever heard of Imposter Syndrome? This is an all-too-common psychological response where you feel inadequate and believe you lack certain skills to succeed. Even if you have succeeded in the past—or are successful now—you may feel you are not up to the task and it's only a matter of time before everyone calls you out as a fake and a phony.

This reaction affects everyone from honor-roll college students to seasoned Wall Street executives to Hollywood stars. Oscar-winner Natalie Portman and Starbucks CEO Howard Schultz have both said at times that they were certain their achievements were the result of some terrible mistake.

Now you might think, "What are they talking about? Of course, they deserved their success? Look how smart and talented they are." But when it comes to you, your analysis of talent is blurry. Everyone else is great, but you're not.

My good friend, Stephanie Cable, is a veterinarian who took over the family business from her father. You might think she would never have to deal with confidence issues like Imposter Syndrome because she was walking into a thriving business that she had known for a long time.

But she too had moments where she questioned her ability, especially when she was just starting out.

In fact, at first, she had a hard time introducing herself as Dr. Cable. "I thought the clients could see right through me, that I had no business taking care of their beloved pet and had the nerve to charge for these services," she says. "I felt young and vulnerable, which hindered me from taking the steps that I knew were required to help the pets. I was timid about recommending warranted diagnostics and therapy because they might be expensive, because I was just a young, veterinarian fresh out of school."

BALANCE: Fake it until you make it. We have all heard this phrase before, and while it may sound somewhat dishonest, there is some merit to it. Faking it does not mean that you are being untruthful about your experience or ability, but rather that you are convincing yourself that given time, your skills (and thus your confidence) will emerge.

BLISS

- **Focus on what you know—and the rest will follow.** Stephanie found there were some aspects of her practice that she was quite good at from the get-go, such as conversing with clients. "For example, some people need extensive amounts of discourse even if it means emphasizing the same points repeatedly. Others need to know where their money is going and demand a guaranteed outcome," she says. By focusing on this particular skill, and understanding what each client wanted and seeing the positive results, she was able to build confidence that she could handle other parts of her practice too. This helped her embrace her title and role as "doctor" because she realized she *did* have the experience and skills to help families and their pets.

- **Have an open dialogue with yourself.** Be honest: What are you good at? Or most comfortable doing? Where have you received praise before? Maybe it is personal communication like with Stephanie. Maybe it is problem solving. Maybe it's organization. When you feel like an imposter, remind yourself of your strengths—what you enjoy the most and what people are confident you are doing well—and do not dwell on your perceived shortcomings.

- **Focus on learning rather than on performance.** With a performance mindset, you see any mistakes as evidence of your underlying limitations. Change your mindset to focus instead on the learning process rather than the immediate outcome. This way your mistakes are not seen as "failures," but rather as ways to improve and excel. As Stephanie's father once told her: "Do not be afraid to make a decision, even if it ends up being wrong. At least it was yours!"

BUSINESS

Not knowing your purpose

If you can't answer the question of why you do something, then you will never have the confidence to carry it out. If you don't believe in your business's purpose or objective, you won't believe in yourself.

When he first ran for Congress as a little-known state senator, Barack Obama was beaten in the Democratic primary by thirty-one points—or as he liked to say, he was "whopped." Even by his own admission, his confidence collapsed and he questioned whether politics was the right path for him. Instead of giving up in the face of such daunting failure, he refocused his attention on what his original purpose for getting into politics was and on what he wanted to accomplish through his political work.

As he said in an interview with Humans of New York, "The thing that got me through that moment, and any other time that I've felt stuck, is to remind myself that it's about the work. Because if you're worrying about yourself—if you're thinking, "Am I succeeding? Am I in the right position? Am I being appreciated?"—then you're going to end up feeling frustrated and stuck."[25]

BALANCE: Redirect your energy. When you feel a lack of confidence coming on, especially during dire times, redirect your attention and energy to your purpose—why you got into your chosen field or what you originally wanted to accomplish. What was it that sparked your fire to succeed? It probably made you excited and bursting with confidence. Write it down. Read it. Memorize it. Keep that in the forefront and keep striving toward that goal. Keep it about "the work."

BLISS

- **Define your purpose.** You can do this fairly easily by doing a brainstorming session with your team. Your team could be family or friends, your partner, or your staff. Try doing a thirty-second exercise by throwing out questions and just having everyone yell out one word that answers that question. For example, "How do our customers benefit from our services?" "Why is it good to work here?" "What do we want to achieve?" Then you can take those words everyone brainstormed and begin refining it into your purpose—what everyone believes about your company's purpose.

BUSINESS

Having trouble standing out

Is there anything more crippling than not being able to express yourself among a sea of competition? You cannot predict when situations to stand out may arise, but are you ready when they do? Probably not. You may be afraid of expressing yourself—to share an idea or opinion—because you are not sure how to say it (or even if you should), so what happens? You clam up and let others have their say.

BALANCE: Practice speaking in public. If you have trouble expressing yourself in meetings or in large groups (a common issue) or negotiating with tough customers, then practice speaking to a smaller audience in a controlled, supported setting where nobody is there to judge or criticize. A perfect example of this is Toastmasters International (www.toastmasters. org). Their clubs help people work on their communication skills, practice, and receive feedback. You begin small and gradually work up to making longer and more detailed speeches and presentations. They can also be safe environments for you to work on spontaneous conversations and dialogue.

BLISS

- **Practice scenarios.** If groups don't work for you, then practice standing where you can see yourself in front of a mirror. I know it sounds strange, but it can really help you gain confidence and adjust your stance and mannerisms before you present in front of people. Even better, you can practice in front of friends or family. These are some examples to try. The goal is to find a way for you to practice that is comfortable for you, so you can find where you need to improve and also what you do well. Work at it and realize that all progress, no matter how small, is a giant step in the right direction.

BUSINESS

Underestimating your expertise

"I don't have the experience." "I can't do that." "I'm not skilled enough." How often have you talked yourself into self-doubt by downplaying your lack of ability? Do you think everyone is an expert in every phase of his or her business? Of course not. People are better at some jobs than others. You may not recognize it, but people look at what you can do, first and foremost, and everyone has expertise or is an expert at something. One way to improve your perception that you do have the necessary skills is to showcase the areas in which you feel the most confident.

BALANCE: Involve your children or family. I previously mentioned how in grade school, I would often lend a hand in my mother's office after school—answering the phones, filing records, and whatever I could do. I got to see my mother in full business action, and I know it gave her great pleasure (and confidence) to explain how her business operated and for me to see how she conducted herself with customers, her employees, and potential new clients. Your children can be wonderful motivators. There is so much doubt and fear you can overcome when it involves your kids. Talk to you children about your work, involve them on some level, and let them see you in action. They no doubt will ask you questions in return and want to understand more.

My children have always been a part of my yoga business. They take classes there, and they sometimes come in with me when I have meetings with the staff. When my older son entered high school, he began working at the front desk. His perspective and care for the studio has been a great experience for us to share. It also gave him a whole new insight into what actually goes on behind the scenes and respect for what was created there. When you share the experiences you have in your business or work with those around you, or with someone who already looks up to you, your confidence will rise.

BLISS

- **Volunteer your efforts.** If you do not have kids, lend your time and expertise to volunteer groups. You have skills that people need, so donate them to causes you support. Much research has touted the various health benefits of volunteering, especially in terms of physiological changes. In fact, a 2013 study in the journal *Psychology and Aging* found an association between volunteerism and a decreased risk of blood pressure, which suggests that devoting your time can help you feel calmer, which is just the right medicine you need for confidence.[26] So teach other people what you know. Use your management skills to organize a project. Showcase your ability to problem solve to fix a problem.

BUSINESS

Lacking support

In the next chapter, I discuss how forming relationships is crucial, whether it's with business contacts, coworkers, or clients. So often we don't have the cheering section we need during a crisis of confidence. During those moments, you need to rely on yourself. You are actually your best motivator. No one knows your situation or understands your fears or anxieties better than you. Use this personal insight to your advantage to build up self-confidence so you can tap into it when it's needed.

BALANCE: Adopt mind games. Outside the business environment, nowhere is self-confidence such a driving force than in the sports world. Pro and Olympic athletes often mention how the physical part of their endeavor can only take them so far. They may have natural talent or a strong work ethic to improve their skills (usually both), but eventually those reach a limit.

So what separates Michael Jordan, Michael Phelps, and Serena Williams from everyone else? Why do they come in first time and again? It's their mental game. Sports psychology is an industry all on its own, but businesspeople can learn a lot from how athletes approach confidence.

At the elite level, success is measured in wins and losses. There is little middle ground. Low self-confidence can kill any opportunity to win. If you are afraid to miss that shot or putt, odds are you will.

One way athletes overcome negative thinking and self-doubt is with visualization—they picture the end result of their success before they even begin. They rehearse the outcome they want in their mind over and over before they do it. As golf great Jack Nicklaus once said, "I never hit a shot, not even in practice, without having a very sharp, in-focus picture of it in my head."

But this is not just thinking about success. They *feel* their success too. They tap into all their senses and imagine all the sensations they experience during competition that correlates with winning.

How does this work for you in the competitive, yet non-athletic, world of business?

Visualize your end success—nailing that presentation, landing that elusive client, leading that project to a glowing success. What are you feeling? Who is nearby? What is the environment like? Picture it over and over so that when it comes time to step up and make it happen, it already has—in your mind.

BLISS

- **Find a mantra.** Muhammad Ali coined the best self-confidence booster of all time whenever he triumphantly announced, hands outstretched overhead in victory, "I am the greatest!" It may have sounded cocky, but when he said it with such force, everyone believed him. When he succeeded in the ring, it just confirmed the obvious. And when he lost, we never doubted his talents. He just climbed back into the ring and competed again (and with even greater success) because he always proclaimed that he was in fact the greatest. We believed Ali was great because he told us. He believed it because he told himself. It all began with a simple mantra, repeated over and over: I am the greatest. When we lose our confidence, a good pep talk is sometimes all we need. Social media is full of inspirational quotes. They get tweeted, pinned, and posted. I often collect some that I find especially motivating. They come from all kinds of people: business leaders, politicians, religious figures, or even anonymous sources. Collect mantras of your own. Keep them short and simple. I keep many of my favorites on my Instagram page (@amyvettercpa): "Beauty is wherever you are at this moment"; "Believe in your vision"; "Look forward not down"; "Life is choices not destiny." When needed, read them again, or better yet, memorize your favorites. When you need to feel great, repeat them to yourself over and over.

- **Strike a pose.** Sometimes your internal mental boost can come from a physical gesture. Harvard Business School professor and social psychologist Amy Cuddy is famous for advocating the "Superman" pose as a way to boost confidence. Her theory is that standing only for a moment with feet apart, hand on hips, chin tilted upward can evoke feelings resembling a superhero, which will "nudge" your mind to produce an instant psychological and behavioral improvement.[27] You look "super" so you feel super. The research supporting this type of body language has been mixed, but it may help you when you need a quick jolt of confidence before a sales meeting or other high-pressure situations.

- **Take a breath.** Taking a really deep breath and exhaling it audibly can work as well. Many times before I speak to a large audience, I get excitement or worry jitters. I find that a series of breathing exercises beforehand can slow down my heart rate and reset my nervous system, so I am ready to go.

B³ BASICS

All successful people will tell you stories about when they faced crippling self-doubt and wondered if they ever would make it. But they kept going. They pushed through failures and downtimes and stayed positive that their efforts would pay off. Here is how you can improve your confidence levels:

- **Don't fear failure.** You may fail more times than you succeed. For every success story, there are hundreds of tales of previous failures. Trying and failing and trying again is part of the process. You must accept that you will not do everything right and you will make mistakes.

- **Know your purpose.** When a lack of confidence hits especially during dire times, redirect your attention and energy to your purpose and why you got into your chosen field or what you originally wanted to accomplish. What was it that sparked your fire to succeed?

- **Improve by practicing.** Embrace your shortcomings for what they are: an opportunity. Work on improving your weakness, but don't approach it as one huge undertaking. Begin small and take steady steps of progress.

- **Don't overthink it.** There are times in both life and business when ignorance is bliss. The less you know or think about a situation and just go with your instinct without overthinking it, the better off you will be.

- **Enlist a support staff.** Depending on your position and your needs, forming a supportive staff where you can outsource certain tasks and responsibilities can help carve out the extra time you need for more crucial tasks without being buried in details.

B³ BRAINSTORMING

B³ BRAINSTORMING

_____

_____

_____

_____

_____

_____

_____

_____

_____

_____

_____

_____

_____

_____

_____

_____

_____

_____

_____

_____

5

THE POWER OF PERSONAL CONNECTION

Business relationships for every kind of personality

Fortune 500 companies have advisory boards stocked with gifted professionals who offer their expertise, insight, and advice on how the business should operate. All board members have different skills and perspectives, and their goal is to help the company succeed, because when the company succeeds everyone benefits.

You need to think of yourself as a potential Fortune 500 company too and surround yourself with your own advisory board.

Everyone needs guidance at some time. It does not matter whether you are starting your first job or are a seasoned CEO. You cannot go through your entire business career (and life) without needing someone to offer sage advice, helpful suggestions, or to just listen while you try to sort out your problems. In essence, you need your own advisory board.

How we cultivate our advisory board, however, depends on our needs—and to a degree, our gender.

People rely on friendships for different reasons. For women, friendships can be a way to get through stressful times, according to a UCLA study.[28] The researchers found that women can react to stress differently than men do and release more of the hormone oxytocin as part of their response to stress. (Men don't release much of the hormone and instead rely on the fight-or-flight response to combat stress.) Oxytocin is the so-called "love" or bonding hormone, which may motivate women to seek out female friendships during stressful times whether in life or in business.

Men's relationships—and business networking—tend to revolve around their primary role as hunter and provider. It's not that women don't fill those roles too, but for men their initial instinct is to build business networks that help them in business first because that is how they succeed and provide. These kinds of business relationships are called transactional relationships because they focus on the business of doing business. If a friendship develops, that is great, but it is not often the primary motivation.

This is one reason I think men often travel in "packs." In my experience, I find that they seem more comfortable in a group setting where there is less one-on-one time, whether it's meetings, playing a round of golf, or attending a sports event. When a business relationship is based on a transaction, the relationship can end at its completion, only to pick up again during the next business encounter. I have seen men bring their packs, which they have developed over time, from job to job, because they know that with those people around them, they are more likely to succeed.

Women, on the other hand, often gather and "collect" relationships. Women realize the importance of acquiring friends and understand how these relationships take time to develop. Yes, women enjoy social groups, but they come to cherish their individual friendships.

In business, many women have difficulty establishing business friendships like they have in their personal lives, and thus they do not network as easily as men. This may be because of all the other demands placed on women in their personal and work lives, which can cause them to be laser focused on getting their work done but spend less time building relationships to create their "pack" inside an organization.

Yet, there may be another underlying issue at play. In my experience and in discussions with many professional women, I have found that they have a tougher time because there is an undercurrent of women not helping each other in business. In short, many women often view other women as a potential threat rather than as allies.[29]

I experienced this in my first job. A senior manager in a firm where I worked pulled me aside one day and said "successful women don't look like you." As a career-minded young woman—at my first job and quite impressionable—this crushed me. I went to my car and cried. The following day, I put a plan in action to change everything about my appearance, in case that was what everyone was thinking, as she had inferred. After months of not feeling like myself, but trying to change because of what she had said, I discovered that no one else in the firm had ever said anything like that. This had only come from her. I will never know her real intentions for giving me this "advice." I quickly learned how hard it was to succeed as a woman in business with so many barriers to overcome.

In my travels, I meet successful women throughout the accounting and technology industry every day. One senior woman manager shared a story with me on how she was spearheading an initiative in her firm to create an environment and culture to bring more women into leadership.

This woman was being considered for partnership at the time. She found herself alone at a table full of male leaders. She took it upon herself to fight for women's initiatives in her firm. She found that the men supported it as a political issue, but it wasn't necessarily coming from their hearts. Layering onto that, the women in the firm were not making it easy for her to help them. She overheard some of the women who worked part-time talking about her one day. They were rooting *against* her because, in their minds, if she made partner it would ruin the chances for a partnership path for all the women who had reduced schedules.

These women were falling into a pattern found in many businesses, but it is often not spoken about. Many women think that there are only so many positions available for women in a company and, if they don't get one—then that's it, the door has closed and more slots won't be available for them later. If more women earn leadership positions, it actually benefits ALL women in the company because those women can then bring in other women when leadership positions become available.

I know it may sound as if I'm over simplifying how women and men socialize in business. Of course, not all women—myself included—are as I describe. I know hundreds of women who excel at business friendships and creating business networks, but I think, more times than not, this is an area where women need to improve. I believe it's just not discussed because many of us are afraid to speak up about it and of the possible backlash that would ensue.

Men are not immune to this either. The "pack" can often be dominated by strong-willed and overpowering personalities, which makes it difficult to create any type of bond. Plus, that type of setup may not work for your personality, and you may be more comfortable with less competition and in a less intimidating environment.

Even if you have no trouble with business friendships and are great at networking, it may not be enough. Again, you need a complete advisory board that includes all kinds of people with backgrounds that can address your potential needs now and down the road.

You will always have questions—When should you ask for a raise? How should you deal with a difficult coworker or troublesome project? You may need guidance on your next career move or updates on new opportunities. Other times, you just need someone with whom to consult and talk. Your advisory board can offer you this support and guidance when you need answers.

Choose Your Advisory Board to Complement Your Personality

Businesses succeed because they are made of different personalities with different skills. You need all kinds of people—including introverts, extroverts, and some combination of the two.

For some people, developing an advisory board through personal connections is easy, but for others it can be an overwhelming task. Both types of personalities have their strengths, weaknesses, and their challenges.

You don't want to change your personality to match your advisory board but rather to embrace it. Recognize your personality for its strength and value. Then you can better approach how to cultivate the relationships that you need—at home, at work, and in your personal life. This will also improve your relationships with people whose personalities don't mesh with yours. How often have we misread someone because of who we *think* they are—instead of trying to better understand who they actually are?

First let's take a closer look at the two main personality types: introverts and extroverts. Most people probably identify themselves as one of these, but knowing the difference between these types, and what they each offer, can help you better cultivate relationships.

INTROVERTS

Most people probably know whether they are an introvert. Here is a look at some of the telltale signs from Susan Krauss Whitbourne, PhD, a professor of psychology at the University of Massachusetts Amherst[30]:

1. **You enjoy time to yourself.** When you take a break you often read, listen to music, or choose other similarly isolated activities.

2. **Your best time for thinking happens when you are alone.** Introverts are not against team meetings or group brainstorming sessions, but they find their best ideas when they are alone with their thoughts.

3. **You usually are the last person to raise your hand.** It's not that introverts know less than others; they just don't feel a need to always share their insight with others.

4. **You don't offer your opinion—others have to ask for it.** Introverts are not quick to share their thoughts, opinions, or advice in a group.

5. **You receive more calls and emails than you send out.** You are not the first person to generate communication but instead react to what you receive from others.

6. **You don't engage in small talk.** Chat with a stranger or casual acquaintance? Not if you can help it.

Introverts may think they are at a distinct disadvantage in the business world, but their personality actually has many benefits and valuable skills that companies need to succeed. Here is what introverts can offer:

They are not into the drama. Introverts are interested in creating something. This means they often don't get pulled into company politics or soap operas where people vie for attention or recognition, which as we all know, can be a distraction from attending to the daily needs of the business.

They are great thinkers. Introverts are not always shy—some are rather outgoing—but they usually process their information and energy internally, which is why they prefer small groups or alone time to function. The upside—this allows them more time to brainstorm, think, research, and analyze problems and then come up with strategies.

They don't need much praise. Introverts tend to rely on their own inner compass to know whether they are doing a good job. This makes them valuable because they can take a concept and run with it—with little, if any, affirmation. It's not that they don't need praise, or don't benefit from it, but it is not a driving force for them.

They're better listeners. Introverts may keep to themselves, but that doesn't mean they are not aware of their surroundings. They listen, think, and process what they hear, and then only speak when they have something to say. As a result, introverts often make surprising connections because they're more focused on information input than output.

Many times the best businesspeople aren't the best talkers; they're the best listeners. They are the ones who ask the right questions at the right time.

BUSINESS

You are an introvert

As I've shown, this is not necessarily a "problem," but an introverted personality can keep you from cultivating relationships and creating the advisory board you need. It may not seem important, but trust me, you need strong bonds with others in business and in life.

BALANCE: Find a Mentor. If you are not good at meeting people and building relationships, you need to enlist a mentor. This is someone who can help you be more successful in your job. This person often has more experience in the company and could be a higher-level individual (but not always) who knows the ropes and can offer advice and guidance to help you grow in your position. A mentor is also someone you share your frustrations and bad days with like any friend socializing over Happy Hour drinks.

When I moved to South Florida from Cincinnati, I interviewed for a job and immediately wanted the woman who conducted the interview to be my friend. We just clicked right away. She was the ideal mentor for me because she was above me position-wise and would not be a competitor for future jobs. She knew all the ins and outs of the operation and how everything ran. When I started that position, and throughout my time there, she gave me tips on how certain meetings ran and how to prepare for them. She gave me comparable stories on different people in the organization so I could present myself in the right light. In addition, we formed a friendship where we helped each other build trust in one another.

Mentors can also be helpful when you confront confidence issues, and they can sometimes elevate you to situations where you can work to express yourself. Kimberly Ellison-Taylor, chairwoman of the American Institute of CPAs (AICPA) Board of Directors, has long benefitted from mentorships during her career. During her early career at the NASA Goddard Space Flight Center, she experienced one of her most memorable mentorship relationships with a manager.

"There was an opportunity to present the status of an initiative to his boss's boss. The request came to him, and I was delighted to help with the preparation," she says. "But imagine my surprise when he said, 'Kimberly, you are doing the presentation.' He sat at the table while I stood at the front and gave me encouraging nods during my presentation. Who does that? His actions not only showed me what I was capable of, confidence-wise, but also shaped my perspectives on mentorship, leadership, delegation, and how to empower team members as my career grew."

This shows the range of input and guidance that mentors can offer and how your relationship with mentors can broaden your experience in ways you may find difficult to accept. In the end, mentorships offer benefits that can have a long-lasting impact.

To create a stronger relationship, it is not always what mentors can do for you but what you can do for them to give back. Early when meeting someone new, I have a strong sense of determining that person's personality type from his or her body language or tone of voice. I quickly learned from my mentor that her skill in recognizing personalities was not as sharp as mine. My mentor offered me the context that I needed to be successful, and I provided her with my insights on different people—we were mutually able to help each other. The promise to your mentors to give future help—when it is needed—can be enough to convince them to devote their time and energy to your relationship.

For women, this type of engagement can be especially beneficial. A 2015 study from the University of California, looked at 139 high-potential employees at a software development lab for a US-based company in China. The researchers reported that women gained more social capital from a connection with a mentor than the men did.[31]

Businesses can profit too. For example, studies have explored business-sponsored mentoring programs and consistently found that they build employee loyalty by showing a willingness to invest in their growth and development. The programs also create a more positive work environment, which can translate to greater productivity and help groom people for future advancement.

More businesses offer mentoring programs. If yours doesn't, ask your human resources department about it. You can also establish one of your own. Here's how.

Ask yourself what you want in a mentor. Do you need an expert who can help you with a specific business challenge, such as asking for a promotion or how to better present yourself? Do you want an at-work person with knowledge of company dynamics, or a person on the outside who can offer you more general counsel? Kimberly Ellison-Taylor suggests using the Strengths, Weakness, Opportunities, and Threats (SWOT) analysis to find the gap between where you are and where you want to be. (A sample

SWOT exercise can be found at www.amyvetter.com/resources.) The results can help identify your personal gaps to determine who best can mentor you to develop those opportunities so that you have positive outcomes.

Choose someone you can trust. A mentor is someone you can confide personal matters to during trying times. You want someone who won't see you as a rival or who has a position that might overlap with yours. Do not reach out to someone you don't know or trust. Mentors need to be people to whom you have already shown your potential, they should have a vested interest in your success, and they should like and trust you already.

Consider a mentor who is younger than you. You might want to tap a younger mentor who offers more experience and guidance when it comes to new fields and areas like technology. This doesn't have to be a formal mentorship. For example, I purposely hire younger staff at my yoga studio and assign them tasks, such as social media, to see what they come up with. Their ideas on things we should do in the business are completely different from mine because they have a different point of reference on communication preferences for their generation. Being open to listening to those ideas and combining them with your experience can be a win-win.

Avoid the formal request. If there is not a formal program at your place of business, the "Will you be my mentor?" approach can be uncomfortable and puts all the pressure on the potential mentor. Begin by simply asking for advice about something and gauge your prospective mentor's reaction. Are they open and willing to offer advice and was it helpful? As you both get comfortable with this approach, reach out about him or her being a formal mentor. That is how it worked with my mentor. We first established a strong friendship that eventually grew into a mentor-mentee relationship.

Build relationships with multiple mentors. It's rare to get through your career with only one mentor. In fact, many people have several at one time, or different ones throughout their career. Your network can be as large or small as you want, but sometimes it can be helpful to get a variety of perspectives.

Don't think mentoring is only for people just starting out. There are many points on everyone's career path when you need mentoring. As your career changes, so do your needs. Mentoring doesn't have to be a business relationship. Depending on your goals, you can find mentors outside the workplace. "Mentors are everywhere," says Kimberly Ellison-Taylor. "They are in your family, your neighborhood, the grocery store."

BLISS

- **Show your gratitude.** Mentoring can sometimes feel like a one-way street—you asking something from your mentor and not doing anything in return. Even mentors with the best intentions, may feel taken advantage of if you just bombard them with requests for help all the time. So always make sure to show your appreciation. The relationship needs to go both ways. Show your gratitude by serving as a source of support for your mentors. You may not be able to offer professional guidance, but you can be someone they can confide in when they go through rough patches. You can also help them on projects or communicate positive comments to other coworkers or management to help them succeed. Mentorship is an energy-boosting opportunity for both of you. Even regular interaction with no agenda is a good way to keep the relationship strong. Schedule regular get-togethers where you just visit, and not only talk about business but also have casual conversations about work and life.

- **Volunteer for professional organizations.** Tom Hood, CEO of the Maryland Association of CPAs (MACPA), says that joining a professional organization is an ideal way to find mentors—either your primary or supplementary ones. When he began his accounting career, he joined the MACPA and was encouraged to volunteer for some committees. He found it helped support the organization, and it exposed him to other CPAs with whom he probably would not have interacted. When he joined the Electronic Data and Work Processing Committee at the MACPA, it connected him with other leaders of the association who became an extension of his personal advisory board. "They say when you volunteer, you get what you put into it, but my volunteering with MACPA showed me you get ten times what you put into it," he explained. "Ever since that first experience, I have used volunteering to develop the trusted relationships to be my ad hoc personal advisory boards and mentors."

• **Be a mentor yourself.** The people you reach out to also get something back. For instance, a 2013 study in the *Journal of Vocational Behavior* looked at five career outcomes for mentors: job satisfaction, organizational commitment, turnover intent, job performance, and career success. The researchers found that mentoring produced the following results:

1. Mentors were more satisfied with their jobs and committed to the company.

2. Providing role-modeling, mentoring was most associated with improved job performance.

3. Mentoring quality was linked with greater mentor career success[32].

• **Work with introverts.** Whether you work with introverts or they are part of your team, you should follow some basic guidelines that can help everyone work better together. For instance, communicating via email as much as possible gives introverts the space and uninterrupted time to get their thoughts together. Be sure to listen when they do speak, because they often put a lot of thought into what they want to say, so odds are it's important. Do not be offended if they seem antisocial and rebuff after-hour gatherings. You might see it as a bonding moment, but they do not. Finally, give introverts plenty of time (and outline objectives) before group meetings; they usually do not do well with last-second meetings and need time to process and plan.

EXTROVERTS

Some estimates suggest extroverts make up 75 percent of the population, so odds are if you are not one, you work with them. Extroverts' brains are literally wired differently than introverts' brains, which may explain their behavior. In fact, one study from the National Cancer Institute found that people identified as extroverts have a longer D4DR gene on Chromosome 11. What does that mean? The researchers found that this change makes them less sensitive to dopamine (the reward and pleasure neurotransmitter) that the brain produces. Therefore, they have to get more external stimulation to make up for it.[33] (On the flipside, introverts have a shorter D4DR, which means their brains are more easily satisfied by dopamine and they don't need more stimuli.)

The average extrovert has a lot to offer a business, and like introverts, you need them on your team. In many ways, they are simply the opposite of introverts. For instance, extroverts are energized by social contact. They thrive on meeting and conversing with people. This makes them ideal for getting and maintaining clients, which is why they are so valuable for damage control when it comes to confrontations.

They usually succeed as the voice for large brainstorming sessions and generate ideas by talking out loud with a group of people. Extroverts are also good at connecting the dots. They can take in information and then spit it back out to form a quick opinion, which is ideal when projects or daily business gets stuck or loses direction. They are always looking for ways to move forward and improve, and they like to encourage more social interactions such as networking, attending seminars, and training.

BUSINESS

You are an extrovert

You may think extroverts would have no problem forming personal relationships and creating their advisory board. For the most part that is true. But while extroverts are good at communicating and connecting with people, they sometimes don't form tight bonds, especially when it comes to supporting their career. They may know a lot of people but may not know any people very well.

BALANCE: Get a Sponsor. A sponsor is similar to a mentor in that you establish a one-on-one relationship with an individual, but this type of interaction is not as personal. A sponsor tends to be ideal for extroverts because this relationship focuses on networking and connections, which taps into the extroverts' natural impulse when it comes to relationships.

With your sponsor, you don't share personal matters or talk about your frustrations or uncertainties. He or she is often a senior-level person who is connected and well grounded in your company or industry. Sponsors take you under their wing and help groom you for a leadership position or help lift you to the next opportunity.

Sponsorships are not something you choose; instead, they are chosen for you. How you get matched with a sponsor depends on you. Most senior-level managers and executives are always on the lookout for talent. They constantly cultivate a working list of people who could move up if certain needs or situations arise, so you want to be on that list.

You want to grab attention and stand out whenever you can. This doesn't mean you have to be the ultimate people pleaser or suck up. Instead, the best way to secure a sponsorship is to be noticed, and if you are not noticed, work up the guts to ask someone how you can be. Stay diligent in your work and career, and leaders will want to help you. Believe me, when you do good work, it gets noticed by the right people. But you must earn it.

Many of my roles in corporations have stemmed from executives seeing me speak or finding out about the work I have done from a mutual customer or person we know. Many times I was unaware I was on their radar, but because they took notice, when an opportunity arose, they thought of me. This has helped me tremendously to grow into new positions and opportunities—and to be challenged, so that I can learn more. Most of my positions in companies have happened organically by networking and building relationships rather than working through job hunters or recruiters. Generally, when people stick their necks out to sponsor you and bring you into the organization, they are more appropriate to help you succeed, because it is a reflection on them as well. Take notice and look around—whether it's at meetings, via social media, or in other ways—to determine what contacts you have and how you may be able to help each other. Even more important, do good work and make your sponsor look good.

Once you find a sponsor, that person can provide advice to assist you in doing your current job better. At one of the companies where I worked, they sold their product a certain way. I decided to take a new approach, based on my experience with running my own business previously. I believed that this new sales approach would improve the experience for the customer segment the company was targeting. I got a lot of pushback from upper management, but my sponsor stood up for me. He told me, "Let me handle their objections. I understand your approach and will support you. Just keep doing what you are doing."

The key here was that I got his buy-in on my approach first. He provided feedback and recognized that the company would benefit if my approach succeeded. I didn't make this decision on my own and break from the norm without management support. He was willing to take a risk because he believed in my skills and proven track record—he also knew it would reflect positively on him if it all worked out. Luckily the gamble paid off and we all benefitted in the end.

Obtaining a sponsor on a certain timeline can often be hard to predict. Sponsors are not people who are as easy to find as mentors, so they are not usually your first target for building your advisory board. Nonetheless, they are essential, and you should always be on the lookout for a potential sponsor opportunity.

BLISS

- **Sponsor.** Sponsorship relationships are also a two-way street. I know, because I have been sponsored and have been a sponsor. When people go out of their way to be successful as a leader and on the job; as a sponsor, I am motivated to help them with future opportunities. Above all else, I look for work ethic, care for the customer, and passion for the business. When people demonstrate these competencies, I am always looking for opportunities to help them. What can you do to improve yourself and show value to your sponsor and the company? Could you aspire to extra accreditation or learn more about parts of the company outside your direct area of expertise?

- **Work with extroverts.** As with introverts, the key to working with extroverts is to focus on their strengths and let them do more of what their personality craves by feeding their constant need for external input. Assign extroverts to group work, team lead, and customer-facing positions. Capitalize on motivational strengths by putting them in charge of committees. If you have information to relay to your staff and would like the message emphasized further, put your extroverted staff member to work spreading the word.

BUSINESS

You are a little bit of both: introvert and extrovert

Some people are a combination of both, called ambivert, where they move back and forth between the two, sometimes with no obvious reason. A 2013 study in the journal *Psychological Science* suggests that two-thirds of people don't strongly identify as either introverts or extroverts.[34]

BALANCE: Get a Coach. Growing up we all had idols. Maybe they were sports figures, celebrities, or even rock stars. We followed their lives and looked up to them as role models. Sometimes as we get older we leave our idols behind. However, this is when we need them the most.

In my career, which has consisted of owning businesses as well as being an executive at several large companies, much of what I have accomplished I owe to my role models, but now I call them "coaches." They have coached me in the skills I needed to succeed.

This part of your advisory board is ideal—no matter your personality type—because you can control who you choose for your coach (or coaches), what you need from them, and your level of interaction—from a close relationship to a distant one.

Coaches can be people we admire from afar or someone we hire to help us improve certain skills, just like an athlete would. We read their books and blogs, watch their TED Talks, and follow them on social media. We may never have a chance to meet many of these people, but they still can play an important role in our lives. We look to them for education, inspiration, and guidance.

Coaches can be regular people, friends, or relatives. For Stephanie Cable, the veterinarian who took over the family practice from her father, one of her early coaches was her dad. He taught her many of the basics for success as she entered the veterinarian business, and he was there whenever

she needed assistance. For instance, he helped her understand the importance of being your own boss, especially as a woman in business.

"For the first couple of years, I was just a vet getting to know the profession, but when the everyday practice became more comfortable, he eased
me into other aspects of running the business. One day he said, 'Let's pay
some bills.' Little by little, I took on additional responsibilities so I gained
an understanding of what it took to own and take pride in the business."

In my early years, I remember learning from my grandmother Edith
and great Aunt Charlotte. Edith was the first person I knew who owned
a business (an antique store) during a time when not many women did.
She wore pants instead of skirts and traveled alone, which was unheard of
for women at the time. Additionally, I heard stories about my Great Aunt
Charlotte who attended business school at the University of Minnesota in
1930, when not many women were represented in business, let alone pursu-
ing higher education.

These stories instilled in me at an early age the importance of striving
for whatever you want even if it is outside the norm. I always look to Edith
and Charlotte to remind me to always pursue my dreams no matter the
obstacle and to live my life on my terms.

When I was in middle school, my mom gave me a huge book to
read—*The Fountainhead* by Ayn Rand. Rand wrote about powerful women
characters in business in the 1940s, long before women could actually
accomplish what she wrote about. Her books inspired me from a young
age and showed that it was possible for a girl to accomplish anything with
hard work and a vision, which I believe gave birth to my ability to spear-
head my own path. I still pick up Rand's books and read passages for a
gentle reminder of the strength of perseverance from those characters when
I get stuck.

My coach, for most of my upbringing, was my mother. I learned skills
I would eventually need to be an entrepreneur by watching my mother gain
experience in her business. Throughout my career, I have found there are

always times to pause and bring in a coach when necessary. I have hired business coaches along the way to help me assess where I am in my career and get some outside guidance on skills I need to progress to the next level, whether those are soft or occupational skills.

Who are the coaches in your life? To determine this, ask yourself: Who inspires me and why? What can you learn from them? Begin making a list of people you would consider for a personal coach, or research potential outside business coaches, to help you fill your own gaps and keep you moving forward at each stage of your career. This part of your advisory board is the easiest to form because you don't have to rely on others and you can personalize it yourself.

BLISS

- **Look outward.** Access potential coaches where they spend time—such as social media groups, their blog, or at conferences. Review their most inspiring speeches and have their books on hand with favorite passages underlined or highlighted so that you can easily refer back to them. Find business coaches and make the investment in yourself. Often we wait for our place of work to provide them, but we should be proactive. This is a lifelong process that benefits you—it's worth the time and money to seek coaches to help you continue to identify gaps or find areas where you are stuck and then create your improvement plan.

B³ BASICS

An advisory board can benefit everyone at any stage of his or her career. Choosing members of your board—whether it is a mentor, sponsor, or coach, or some combination of the three—is often based on your needs and personality type.

- **You need your own advisory board.** Everyone needs guidance at some time whether you are starting your first job or you are a seasoned CEO. You cannot go through your entire business career (and life) without needing someone to offer sage advice, helpful suggestions, or to just listen while you try to sort out your problems.

- **Choose your advisory board to complement your personality type**—whether you are an introvert, extrovert, or some combination of the two.

- **Find a mentor if you are an introvert.** A mentor is someone who helps you be successful in your job and is ideal for introverts who have difficulty meeting people and building relationships. A mentor often has more experience in the company and could be a higher-level individual (but not always) who knows the ropes and can offer advice and guidance to help you grow in your position.

- **Get a sponsor if you are an extrovert.** A sponsor is similar to a mentor in that you establish a one-on-one relationship with an individual, but this type of interaction is not as personal. A sponsor tends to be ideal for extroverts because this relationship focuses on networking and connections, which taps into the extroverts' natural impulse when it comes to relationships.

- **Get a coach if you are combination.** This part of your advisory board is ideal—no matter your personality type—because you can control who you choose for your coach (or coaches), what you need from them, and your level of interaction. This can range from a close relationship to a distant one. Coaches can be people we admire from afar or someone we hire to help us improve certain skills, just like an athlete would. We read their books and blogs, watch their TED Talks, and follow them on social media. We may never have a chance to meet many of these people, but they still can play an important role in our lives. We look to them for education, inspiration, and guidance.

B³ BRAINSTORMING

B³ BRAINSTORMING

_____

_____

_____

_____

_____

_____

_____

_____

_____

_____

_____

_____

_____

_____

_____

_____

_____

_____

_____

_____

6

APPLYING THE B³ METHOD

Strategies to help you and your business succeed

Now that you have seen how the B³ Method came to be and how you can use it to create the work-life harmony you need; you might ask yourself—How do I begin?

Change takes some amount of faith and even courage. Yet, often the first step to overcoming any initial hesitation is believing we have the brainpower to do so. We tend to think there is a limit to what our brains can do. The reality is that everyone's brain has the capacity to continue to grow and learn new things at almost any age.

It is a process called neurogenesis—where new neurons (brain cells) develop in the hippocampus, the brain region responsible for learning new information. Research has suggested that many activities that are common in a person's chosen Balance can activate this reaction.

For instance, one study in the April 1, 2016, *Journal of Physiology* suggests that moderate-intensity exercise like jogging, power walking, or swimming might help generate more hippocampal neurons than would be generated when not doing any kind of activity.[35]

Other research suggests that doing brain exercises, which make you focus your attention, can have a similar effect in the hippocampus. In fact, research published in the *Journal of Neuroscience* found that playing complex video games—a possible Balance activity—where you need to learn and recall more information—improves memory performance by 12 percent compared with memory in people who played simpler video games.[36] The researchers speculate that any kind of similar activity that encourages intense concentration, such as music and painting for example, can have the same effect.

So don't think for an instant that you are incapable of trying to change how you think, how you work, or how you live. The only limitation you have for change is you, or your preconceived notions of what you can and cannot do. Your brain is actually capable of expanding into new areas if you take the chance to see what is possible.

Implementing the B³ Method in Your Life

Remember that your Balance is the foundation for the B³ Method. Your chosen Balance is a personal decision. Keep in mind that it may be a work in progress. Do not worry if you struggle at first with finding the right one and then being able to follow it through in the face of daily life challenges. The most important thing is that you make a commitment to change and then you can take the steps to get there that are right for you.

All the stories, research, and scenarios in this book have offered a way to identify the areas where you need the most focus at this point in your life. The B³ Method is also designed to help in everyday situations. When you encounter an uncomfortable moment in work or in life, take a breath, and apply the B³ methodology: Business, Balance, and Bliss.

- **Business:** First, stop and assess the situation. Define your scenario so that you can clearly articulate what needs to happen to reach a solution.

- **Balance:** Next, apply techniques from the chosen Balance in your life to the business situation to create a better outcome. You may have to try different activities to find the right Balance for you, so make sure you are flexible and open to making adjustments.

- **Bliss:** Last, once you find a Balance that works to resolve the Business situation, make a commitment to sustain the change you've accomplished. It could be something as simple as implementing calendar appointments, or reaching out for support from family and friends. Use something that helps you learn to make your Balance a habit, rather than a short-term fix.

Sometimes, the main obstacle in finding your Balance is that we choose the wrong kind despite our good intentions. We seek out Balance in ways that do not meet our real needs.

For example, every January without fail my yoga business and the gyms/fitness centers across the country enjoy a healthy spike in new memberships. The reason is obvious—for many people, a new year is the ideal opportunity to change how they live. New year, new you—people buy into the hype proclaimed by so many magazine covers.

People's desire to change often revolves around many personal issues, but one of the strongest motivations is physical. They want to lose weight and get in shape. They also see exercise as a way to burn off stress. The idea is that if they look better and feel better, they will be happier and that will carry over to other aspects of their life, including their work.

They are striving for Balance. Sounds perfectly reasonable, and generally it is. But what happens within weeks for most of these inspired gym-goers? They stop going.

It has been estimated that the New Year's resolution gym crowd drops off by 80 percent the second week of February. 80 percent!

Do these people start to think their self-improvement goal is no longer worthy? Nope. Do they think they can get their fitness elsewhere? Probably not. Are they no longer motivated? I doubt it.

The problem could be related to a lack of discipline to go to the gym several times a week or to always make the Wednesday night Zumba class. Maybe people don't have a detailed plan on how to reach their goals and they try to wing it, which never turns out well.

Let's take a step back and analyze this sign-up-and-drop-out trend more closely. The question we need to ask is: *Why* the gym?

Why do people think the gym is the key to finding their Balance? I bet if you questioned a lot of people about why they join a gym, they would say, "That's where you go to work out." They simply follow the leader and don't have a personal attachment to why they are doing it. There is much research to support this thinking.

Some behavioral economists believe our brains are hardwired to be locked into commitments like a gym contract. We may fight other long-term commitments like cell phones, but gym memberships tend to be an exception. It is part of what these economists call "pre-commitment." The idea is that if you invest in something—in this case a monthly fee—you are more likely to stick with it. After all, you are paying for the gym access and want to get the most out of your money. But of course, most people do not do that.

Don't get me wrong—gyms are great. They provide the necessary equipment and machines and classes and trainers to help you. Many gyms are quite accessible and have flexible hours. You can visit them almost any time, so they fit many types of schedules. For many people, it is the ideal place to find their Balance.

Is the gym the right place for *you?* Do you really enjoy going to the gym or that particular class or plodding along on a treadmill watching TV? Does it excite you or satisfy your interests? Does it make you happy?

While many people may recognize the need for Balance, they go about it the wrong way. They choose what is easiest or most convenient or what other people think they should do rather than searching for what is innately natural to them. They focus on the result—if I go to the gym then I'll feel better—instead of the primary motivation of what makes them happy.

Always keep in mind that finding your Balance is a journey that may change over time. That is okay. Be open to that and what comes up for you.

As I discussed earlier, finding your true Balance can sometimes be a simple process because it's what comes natural to you, but if that's not the case for you, here is an approach that may help.

Identify three activities that you enjoy and set aside time on your calendar to explore each one. Schedule it like an appointment—an appointment with yourself. For thirty days, devote a certain amount of time each day to doing one of the interests on your list. Just start with one, don't try to take on too much. As you pursue each one, journal about the experience each day to track your progress and gauge your interest. You may find that in the beginning it's uncomfortable, but as you make an effort, you may begin to like it. For thirty days, journal the following:

- What do you like and why?

- What don't you enjoy and why?

- How do you feel before and after?

After thirty days, try your next interest. And then the next one. After ninety days, decide which of the three didn't feel like work. Focus on the one that you looked forward to doing and that left you feeling better afterward. Make the commitment to continue. We can get discouraged during the learning process, but it takes some time to form a new habit. Try and try again. Eventually you will find where you need to be. Trust the process.

Sometimes when you find your Balance it may not be easy to adopt. What do you do then? As I mentioned, I began a yoga practice and learned to play the guitar, but I also wanted to begin painting again. I was stuck— do I need to go back to school to learn how? Do I need formal lessons? Where do I begin?

I met an artist at an auction whose style I immediately connected with. His paintings inspired me. I asked him what steps I should take to get back into painting again.

His answer was simple. "Get in your car, drive to the art supply store, buy paint and a canvas, and then pick up your brush and paint."

Duh, right? We make the simplest things in life so hard and put up so many hurdles. I did as he said and soon began creating artwork for my yoga studio. It was so fulfilling and empowering.

Your Balance comes down to commitment. Once you have decided which of the interests you want to stick with, set appointments on your calendar. Treat it as if it's a business meeting or an activity for your children, to ensure you set aside the time necessary to turn off work, personal life, and electronics, and just focus on this activity. Just do it! When you make it important; it becomes important.

One of the most important components to changing your path is support. Discuss this new endeavor with your family and/or friends and create a mutual plan of support. Be transparent and explain why you need this—and how it will help everyone else around you—if you improve your well-being.

Your Balance is the best marker for helping you maintain your authentic self. The instant your creative outlet feels like a chore or just another item on your to-do list, then you probably need to find something else.

What about when life happens? Sure, your photography or painting may be your ideal creative outlet, but sometimes even the strongest love and passion for something cannot overcome late nights at the office or home situations that eat into your creative time. That is why we call this work-life harmony.

It ebbs and flows in your life like the rhythm of music. Don't get down on yourself if you miss one time—just know you can make it up the next day, or you may decide it's just not in the cards because of other demands. Either way don't lose your overall vision for maintaining it long term.

This is why you should implement various types of support foundations for your outlet to make sure that it stays in the forefront of your life. Here are some steps to take:

1. **Give yourself permission.** If you think you don't have time for it, kick yourself to take the first step to physically go to the location of your hobby even if it's in your own house. Once you are there, your body, mind, and spirit will thank you. Later, you'll think, "How could I not have made time to refuel myself so I am a better person?" Give yourself the permission to do what you need to for yourself.

2. **Prioritize.** It's really that simple. Participating in a hobby requires you to spend time doing it rather than doing something else. Schedule time for your creative outlet—an hour a day, once a week, every Saturday morning. Schedule it in your calendar, as if it were a work meeting, and stick to it. Soon your outlet will become a ritual and an automatic part of your life.

3. **Find your place.** Set up a separate place in your home—a spare bedroom, corner of the living room, basement, or even your garage. Sometimes you need a sacred space for your outlet where you can get away and just focus on your creativity and not be distracted. Or establish an off-site ritual. For instance, visit a café and spend time sketching or writing. Changing your routine can offer extra incentive to do your creative outlet activity because now you can enjoy two things: creativity and getting away for a while.

4. **Join a group**. You are not alone in your quest to tap into your creativity. Often being part of a community can help you maintain a ritual and keep your creativity flowing. Peter Karpas meets with his fellow comic book collectors once a week. You can do the same. Sign up for a class. Recruit friends and form a book club or arts and crafts event where you rotate to different people's houses.

5. **Bring it into your office**. Always keep part of your outlet on site. Prop up your guitar in the corner, keep a sketchpad and pencils on your desk, and store your knitting bag by your chair. If your outlet is within grasp, you are more likely to reach for it when you find a moment, or need a break in your day.

6. **Let others know about it**. Whether you choose to tell your family or people at work about it, let people know what you are doing so they can support you. At work, when you block off time for your chosen hobby, it's important that people realize it is non-negotiable time and meetings cannot be booked over it. With your family, you may need help at your house or with your spouse to be supportive of you taking this time to pursue what you need to recharge yourself. Being transparent goes a long way, and you may find that the example you set becomes contagious and others around you will follow your example.

Get SMART About Your Balance

You may have heard of a business tool called SMART. It's a project management guide for setting objectives, and it's been widely used for decades. SMART stands for Specific, Measureable, Achievable, Realistic, and Time-bound. It is a guide to help develop measurable goals. The thinking behind SMART is that if a goal is well defined, and there are many tools in place to measure and track its progress, the goal will be easier to achieve.

You can also apply this concept to ensure you stay on track while achieving and maintaining your Balance. A well-defined Balance will make reaching Bliss easier.

Here is how you can follow SMART for your Balance.

First you begin by setting the overall goal for yourself. For example, I want to create and maintain an exercise regimen for the next twelve months. Then, to achieve that goal, you put SMART into place:

- **Specific:** Details matter. You can't just say, "I'm going to take up spinning." That's a great choice for a Balance, but it's not specific enough. What kind of spinning? Where? When? For how long? It needs to be defined. Instead, you could say this: "I'm going to take an hour-long beginners' spinning class at my local gym twice a week, Tuesday and Thursday, from 7 p.m. to 8 p.m." Now it has a clear definition and special details.

- **Measurable:** How can you determine if you are hitting the goal you set in front of you. In the example I began with, your measure is going to classes twice a week. So if you are able to get there two times a week at a minimum, you know you are achieving the goal you set for yourself. This can help you stay motivated as you gain confidence that you can sustain the overall goal of building an exercise regimen.

- **Achievable:** Is your Balance something that is physically available to you? You want to make sure you put objectives in place to meet your goal, such as financial, physical, and mental. Also, ensure you have a support system around you to help when times are tough. For example, if you set the goal to take a spinning class twice a week, ensure you have a gym that is accessible from your work or that's near your home. Also make sure you can make the class times, and if you have kids or other dependents, that you have the support you need either at the gym or at home for them. If you create a goal that is insurmountable, you will get frustrated and give up. So keep it simple.

- **Realistic:** Is this a Balance you can easily adopt? You may already have a means to implement your Balance into your life. This is to double-check that you didn't aim too high, which creates room for failure. If spinning is something you can physically accomplish, or you have the fortitude to one day accomplish an entire class, then you know this a good place to begin. But if you have a bad knee, for instance, then maybe you should step back and determine whether there is another exercise like swimming that may be a better fit. Also, ask yourself if your Balance calls for extra effort on your part. Do you have any physical or financial limitations that could interfere with its regular execution now or down the road?

- **Time-bound:** Make sure that whatever goal you set for yourself has deadlines. So in this example, you would begin January 3 and continue for twelve weeks. After that time, you would go back and reevaluate whether this goal is working and whether you need to make any modifications to achieve it during the next twelve months. Keep these agile, so you can modify them as needed to ensure success.

You can find a template for creating your personal SMART goals at www.amyvetter.com/resources. Use it to_complete this exercise and keep yourself on track.

Bringing the B³ Method into Your Work

If you are a business owner, team manager, or head of a department, there are many ways you can share the B³ Method with your employees.

And you should. An investment in your employees helps create workplace happiness, which can be one of the strongest initiatives for loyalty and productivity. And when your workers are happy, everyone is happy. Additionally, it helps to support your own goals.

Think about what makes us really happy with work. Many people may say more money. But is that true? The conventional wisdom used to be that if you paid people enough, they would be happier and thus more productive. That goes for everyone no matter where they stand on the corporate ladder. But, how long does that happiness last?

It makes sense to a certain degree. Sure, we are happy if we make more money, but does that always ensure a more productive worker? Or team leader? Or senior manager? Not always. Money is always a good initiative, but it is not sustainable.

The key to workplace performance is appreciation and support. When we feel like we matter and our work makes a difference, we are happier. And a happy worker is a better worker and a healthier one.

A study from the University of Warwick found that happiness led to a 12 percent rise in productivity.[37] In fact, these researchers also discovered that companies that invested in support and employee satisfaction succeed in generating happier employees. Look at companies like Adobe, Google, Patagonia, and REI, to name but a few. They continue to be ranked as the top businesses in terms of employee satisfaction because they make it a priority to invest in worker happiness. Just look at some of their perks: healthy, gourmet meals; laundry and fitness facilities; and generous paid parental leave, and on-site childcare.

My husband's employer, Ultimate Software, a global technology company with more than 3,700 employees offers similar benefits, such as 100 percent employer-paid health care; paid maternity, paternity, and adoption leave; and two paid service days a year for employees to volunteer at nonprofits of their choosing.

Ultimate is also an enabler of promoting balance in the workplace. To help combat employee stress, they have introduced a mindfulness program—a twelve-week program that meets for hour-long sessions to teach workers how to adopt breathing and meditation exercises that they can apply as needed during their workday. According to Chief People Officer Vivian Maza at Ultimate Software, "In our line of work and current day technology, we are working at all times and can forget to stop and smell the roses. Our work is stressful and demanding and we wanted everyone to try to breathe and focus on the now, which is where we believe mindfulness comes into play."

We can't all be Google or Ultimate Software, but it's not what they offer that matters, but rather that they make an effort so employees care about the work they do beyond a paycheck. These companies show their workers that they want them to be happy when they are on or off the job—and it pays off.

Of course, this makes sense when you step back and examine the psychology of it. When you feel good, you have more energy, the brain fires on all cylinders, you are more willing (and more successful) at fostering relationships and improving communication. You want to interact more. You want to do well. You are motivated to succeed. And you tend to be healthier.

On the flipside, if you are not happy and do not feel appreciated, not only will it affect your well-being and performance, but you are also much more likely to throw in the towel sooner. Both men and women struggle with this problem, but sometimes it can affect women more than it does men.

Take a 2013 study conducted by Pamela Stone, PhD, a sociology professor at Hunter College in New York City. She wanted to pinpoint the struggles of women in the workplace and how those struggles influenced their choices for either staying in the workplace or leaving to stay at home.

Her study looked specifically at high-potential women. These were women who were educated, highly trained, motivated, and in positions of management and leadership. The study discovered that women pursued their careers for an average of eleven years. But the most surprising part was that about 90 percent of these women left the workplace not to begin or devote more time to their family but because of problems in the workplace.[38] The most common complaints were frustration and long hours. The women thought they were pushed out because they felt they could not succeed in that environment and did not feel appreciated.

Even though all of this seems straightforward and follows the science, a direct cause-and-effect result, most companies don't adjust their corporate practices to account for these findings. Or more likely, they do not know how to create employee happiness. That's why it is often up to us to do it for ourselves.

Share Your Balance

Implementing the B³ Method can be one of the best ways to invest in worker satisfaction and happiness. Once you have adopted the B³ Method for yourself and have begun to see and feel the results, you may be inspired to share it with others. The end result—if you feel better, then other people will take notice of the change and want to know how they can make changes in their lives too.

That may sound like a wonderful goal, but you need to approach it in the right way. You don't want to force anything on coworkers or your employees because they may naturally resist. (Think of how you would react if someone said, "You HAVE to try this. Come on I'll show you!")

One way to introduce the B³ Method is to share aspects of your Balance with your people on a small scale. The goal is not to evangelize, per se, but to make it a part of the business atmosphere so everyone can participate on some level. Allow yourself to share your outside of work experiences and newfound passions with your coworkers and team. You may be surprised to learn how that can create a stronger connection with people because you are sharing something personal, and in turn, they may share their hobbies or passions with you.

David K. Williams, CEO of Fishbowl, a company that produces inventory management software, brings his Balance of music into his office with great success. He doesn't force it on other people, but rather his approach is to share what he receives from music with others.

For him, music is about movement and celebration. So when his salespeople hit their numbers, the top two salespeople have a dance off. The company sometimes holds Fishbowl talent shows, where employees are invited to share their musical contributions with others.

For myself, when the people I work with discover I am a yoga instructor, they have many questions about the practice and are interested to learn more about the yoga experience. I have volunteered to teach at the office during lunchtime, at off-site meetings, and conferences. I end up creating a new bond with people I work with when we share a passion for yoga. In fact, many times when coworkers have chosen to take one of my classes, they were motivated to find a nearby studio so they could continue to learn more about yoga.

You could try to do something similar. It's a small step. As your team becomes comfortable with your Balance, then you could introduce stories about how you use it as part of the B³ Method—and how you think it benefits you at work—and see where it leads.

Make It a Contest

It is amazing how a simple reward—along with the initial challenge—can motivate people.

Take the popularity of weight-loss challenges like *The Biggest Loser*. Yes, the people who participate are motivated to lose weight and get healthy, but the real carrot dangling in front of them is the cash prize.

We are motivated to do so much if an award is waiting at the end. Take, for example, this study from the *Journal of the American Medical Association*, which involved overall healthy people with body mass indexes (BMI) of 30 to 40. (BMI is a tool to give an estimate of body fat based on height and weight.) Here, the people were regarded as obese based on their BMI number.

People were split into two groups—one group was offered month-long contracts where they would pay up to $3 per day—and have it matched. After a month, they got all the money back—and thus doubled their investment—but only if they met or exceeded their weight-loss goal. The other group did not get a contract. What happened? You guessed it—the group motivated by money lost an average of fourteen pounds more than the no-contract group.[39]

Money is always a good motivator, but it's usually not the size of the prize that matters but rather the idea. I have known people who sign up for marathons or 5Ks just because they want the finisher medal that everyone gets for completing the race. At my yoga studio, we have something called the Om Club, where people earn "oms" by attending classes. When you have earned one hundred oms, you become a member of the 100 Om Club, receive prizes, and have your name listed in the studio.

With the B³ Method you can do this with some something I call the B³ Challenge. Here, you challenge your team members to find and follow a chosen Balance for thirty days and award prizes for those who hit certain levels—for instance, if they do it for twenty-five to thirty days they get a gift card, and they get a lesser prize for doing it for twenty to twenty-four days, etc.

Have them record what they did, when, and for how long, and then have all participants share their experiences in your weekly team meeting. Create a leaderboard either in the office or virtually so participants know where they stand. Better yet, create a social media account where people can record their interactions, experiences, and maybe even pictures of their Balance for everyone to see and share.

Share Your Bliss

As I have shown, there are many ways to maintain your Balance by using Bliss. You may find some of your favorite ones could easily be introduced into your employee's average workday. For instance, one of my favorite Bliss exercises is pausing for two minutes before entering a meeting to clear my head and organize my thoughts. This can be a great way to begin a team meeting. Before starting a meeting, lead the entire group in a two-minute mindfulness exercise, or set a two-minute alarm and have all attendees close their eyes before the meeting begins. Encourage them to try this before their next personal task or meeting they lead. At a future meeting, ask whether people have used the exercise and how they benefitted. It might open the door for a larger conversation about other types of Bliss and a discussion about the B³ Method in general—what is working for them, what is not working for them, and where they need to modify.

Continue to Grow

Remember that the ultimate goal with the B³ Method is to achieve Bliss and sustain your work-life harmony for yourself as well as for your family, friends, and coworkers. This journey is never a straight line with no obstacles along the way. Things always change in life and in business and you must be ready to move with the ever-changing tides.

The B³ Method is a great tool to remind you to always check in with yourself. Make a point to return to your B³ Brainstorming notes for inspiration and guidance as needed. Come back and review, and possibly re-create your SWOT and SMART goals from time to time to make sure you are still on track—or to determine if you need to alter anything to reflect a new direction in your business career. Add another Balance to your life or find a new one when it makes sense.

Ultimately, once you create B³ habits in your life, the goal is better self-awareness and creating a sustainable work-life harmony for yourself and those around you. In yoga, we call this The Satchitananda (nature of the soul), which broken down means existence, self-awareness, and bliss. This can be your mantra for everyday life. How we each experience these concepts works together to create our inner peace and, eventually, Bliss. My hope for you is that once you deploy the B³ Method in your life and business, in a way that works for you, it can be a constant reminder that everything in life can stand alone, but everything becomes stronger when it all works together.

B³ BASICS

Implementing change like the B³ Method takes time and commitment, but there are strategies on how best to adapt it into your life, help you stay on track, and when the time is right, begin to introduce it into your business.

- **Change often takes some amount of faith and even courage.** Yet, often the first step to overcoming any initial hesitation is believing we have the brainpower to do so. Everyone's brain has the capacity to continue to grow and learn new things at almost any age.

- **The B³ Method is also designed to help in everyday situations.** When you encounter an uncomfortable moment in work or in life, take a breath, and apply the B³ methodology: Business, Balance, and Bliss.

- **Finding your Balance is a journey that may change over time.** Identify three activities that you enjoy and set aside time on your calendar to explore each one. For thirty days, devote a certain amount of time each day to doing one of the interests on your list. As you pursue each one, journal about the experience each day to track your progress and gauge your interest.

- **Use SMART**—Specific, Measureable, Achievable, Realistic, and Time-bound—as a guide to help you develop sustainable measurable goals for your Balance.

- **Invest in people.** Implementing the B^3 Method in the workplace can be a means to invest in employee happiness and satisfaction.

- **Share your personal B^3 stories.** Introduce the B^3 Method through your stories about your personal experiences, sharing Bliss tips, and creating contests and challenges to help motivate people to try it.

B³ BRAINSTORMING

_____

_____

_____

_____

_____

_____

_____

_____

_____

_____

_____

_____

_____

_____

_____

_____

_____

_____

_____

_____

B³ BRAINSTORMING

ENDNOTES

Chapter 2: Finding Your Balance

1   Oswald, A. J., Proto, E., & Sgroi, D. (2015). Happiness and productivity. *Journal of Labor Economics, 33*(4), 789–822. doi:10.1086/681096

2   Kivimäki, M. (2015, October 31). Long working hours and risk of coronary heart disease and stroke: A systematic review and meta-analysis of published and unpublished data for 603 838 individuals. *The Lancet, 386*(10005), 1739–1746. http://dx.doi.org/10.1016/S0140-6736(15)60295-1

3   Nielsen, J. A., Zielinski, B. A., Ferguson, M. A., Lainhart, J. E., Anderson, J. S. (2013) An evaluation of the left-brain vs. right-brain hypothesis with resting state functional connectivity magnetic resonance imaging. *PLoS ONE 8*(8): e71275. doi:10.1371/journal.pone.0071275

4   Himmelman, P. (2015, March 10). Musical skills = entrepreneurial skills. Retrieved March 22, 2017, from http://www.mcareerjuice.com/2015/03/musical-skills-entrepreneurial-skills/

5   The Birkman Method | Leading behavioral & personality assessment. (n.d.). Retrieved March 22, 2017, from https://birkman.com/assessment-solutions/the-birkman-method/

6   Good quality me-time vital for home and work well-being. (2015, January 8). Retrieved March 23, 2017, from http://www.bbk.ac.uk/news/good-quality-me-time-vital-for-home-and-work-well-being; Russell, P. (2015, January 8). Quality 'me time' makes for better workers: Study. Retrieved March 23, 2017, from http://www.webmd.boots.com/stress-management/news/20150108/quality-me-time-study

Chapter 3: Being Present

7   Evans, G. W., & Johnson, D. (2000). Stress and open-office noise. *Journal of Applied Psychology, 85*(5), 779–783. doi:10.1037//0021-9010.85.5.779

8   Kleiman, J. (2013, January 15). How multitasking hurts your brain (and your effectiveness at work). *Forbes.* Retrieved March 22, 2017, from https://www.forbes.com/sites/work-in-progress/2013/01/15/how-multitasking-hurts-your-brain-and-your-effectiveness-at-work/#264754541013

9   Janssen, C. P., & Gould, S. J. (2015, July). Integrating knowledge of multitasking and interruptions across different perspectives and research methods. *International Journal of Human-Computer Studies, 79*, 1–5. http://dx.doi.org/10.1016/j.ijhcs.2015.03.002

10 Mark, G., Gudith, D., & Klocke, U. (2008, April 6). The cost of interrupted work: More speed and stress. Proceedings of SIGCHI Conference on Human Factors in Computing Systems, 107–110. Retrieved from https://www.ics.uci.edu/~gmark/chi08-mark.pdf

11 Too many interruptions at work? (2006, June 8). *Gallup Business Journal.* Retrieved March 22, 2017, from http://www.gallup.com/businessjournal/23146/too-many-interruptions-work.aspx

12 I can't get my work done! How collaboration & social tools drain productivity. (2011, May 18). Retrieved March 22, 2017, from https://harmon.ie/blog/i-cant-get-my-work-done-how-collaboration-social-tools-drain-productivity

13 Saad, L. (2014, August 29). The "40-hour" workweek is actually longer—by seven hours. *Gallup.* Retrieved March 22, 2017, from http://www.gallup.com/poll/175286/hour-workweek-actually-longer-seven-hours.aspx

14 Scheduled overtime effect on construction projects. (2012, January 11). Retrieved March 22, 2017, from http://www.hcgexperts.com/scheduled-overtime-effect-on-construction-projects.php

15 Reid, E. (2015, April 28). Why some men pretend to work 80-hour weeks. *Harvard Business Review.* Retrieved March 22, 2017, from https://hbr.org/2015/04/why-some-men-pretend-to-work-80-hour-weeks

16   Mankins, M. (2016, February 25). Is technology really helping us get more done? *Harvard Business Review.* Retrieved March 22, 2017, from https://hbr.org/2016/02/is-technology-really-helping-us-get-more-done

17   Gouveia, A. (n.d.) 2014 wasting time at work survey. Salary.com. Retrieved March 22, 2017, from http://www.salary.com/2014-wasting-time-at-work/slide/2/

18   New CareerBuilder survey reveals the most common and strangest productivity killers at work. (2015, June 11). CareerBuilder. Retrieved March 22, 2017, from http://www.careerbuilder.com/share/aboutus/pressreleasesdetail.aspx?sd=6%2F11%2F2015&id=pr898&ed=12%2F31%2F2015

19   Schwartz, T. (2013, February 9). Relax! You'll be more productive. *New York Times,* Retrieved March 22, 2017, from http://www.nytimes.com/2013/02/10/opinion/sunday/relax-youll-be-more-productive.html?_r=1

20   Miller, R. (2016, October 18). Learn to listen to your emotions with meditation | Guided meditation. *Yoga Journal.* Retrieved March 22, 2017, from http://www.yogajournal.com/article/meditation-classes/learn-listen-emotions/

21   Boubekri, M., Cheung, I. N., Reid, K. J., Wang, C., & Zee, P. C. (2014). Impact of windows and daylight exposure on overall health and sleep quality of office workers: A case-control pilot study. *Journal of Clinical Sleep Medicine, 10*(6), 603–611. doi:10.5664/jcsm.3780

22   Rahman, S. A., Flynn-Evans, E. E., Aeschbach, D., Brainard, G. C., Czeisler, C. A., & Lockley, S. W. (2014). Diurnal spectral sensitivity of the acute alerting effects of light. *Sleep, 37*(2), 271–281. doi:10.5665/sleep.3396

Chapter 4: Building Confidence

23   Cortese, A., Amano, K., Koizumi, A., Kawato, M., & Lau, H. (2016). Multivoxel neurofeedback selectively modulates confidence without changing perceptual performance. *Nature Communications, 7*, 13669. doi:10.1038/ncomms13669

24   Cech, E., Rubineau, B., Silbey, S., & Seron, C. (2011). Professional role confidence and gendered persistence in engineering. *American Sociological Review,76*(5), 641–666. doi: 10.1177/0003122411420815

25   "When is the time you felt most broken?" (2015, February 06). Humans of New York. Retrieved March 23, 2017, from http://www.humansofnewyork.com/post/110263143446/when-is-the-time-you-felt-most-broken-i-first

26   Sneed, R. S., & Cohen, S. (2013). A prospective study of volunteerism and hypertension risk in older adults. *Psychology and Aging, 28*(2), 578–586. doi:10.1037/a0032718

27   Cuddy, A. (2012, June). Your body language shapes who you are. TED Talks. Retrieved March 23, 2017, from http://www.ted.com/talks/amy_cuddy_your_body_language_shapes_who_you_are

Chapter 5: The Power of Personal Connection

28   Taylor, S. E., Klein, L. C., Lewis, B. P., Gruenewald, T. L., Gurung, R. A., & Updegraff, J. A. (2000). Biobehavioral responses to stress in females: Tend-and-befriend, not fight-or-flight. *Psychological Review, 107*(3), 411–429. doi:10.1037//0033-295x.107.3.411

29   Thibodeaux, W. (2017, March 16). Study finds women interpret looks from one another in the worst ways. Inc.com. Retrieved March 23, 2017, from http://www.inc.com/wanda-thibodeaux/study-women-feel-judged-and-its-not-men-who-are-judging.html?cid=search

30   Whitbourne, S. (2014, March 25). Nine signs you're really an introvert. *Psychology Today.* Retrieved March 23, 2017, from https://www.psychologytoday.com/blog/fulfillment-any-age/201403/nine-signs-you-re-really-introvert

31   Srivastava, S. B. (2015). Network intervention: Assessing the effects of formal mentoring on workplace networks. *Social Forces, 94*(1), 427–452. doi:https://doi.org/10.1093/sf/sov041

32 Ghosh, R., & Reio, T. G. (2013). Career benefits associated with mentoring for mentors: A meta-analysis. *Journal of Vocational Behavior, 83*(1), 106–116. doi:10.1016/j.jvb.2013.03.011

33 Laney, M. O. (2002). In your genes. In *The introvert advantage: How quiet people can thrive in an extrovert world* (pp. 66–67). New York: Workman.

34 Grant, A. M. (2013). Rethinking the extraverted sales ideal. *Psychological Science, 24*(6), 1024–1030. doi:10.1177/0956797612463706

Chapter 6: Applying the B³ Method

35 Nokia, M. S., Lensu, S., Ahtiainen, J. P., Johansson, P. P., Koch, L. G., Britton, S. L. et al. (2016). Physical exercise increases adult hippocampal neurogenesis in male rats provided it is aerobic and sustained. *Journal of Physiology, 594*(7), 1855–1873. doi:10.1113/jp271552

36 Clemenson, G. D., & Stark, C. E. (2015, December 9). Virtual environmental enrichment through video games improves hippocampal-associated memory. *Journal of Neuroscience, 35*(49), 16116–16125. doi:https://doi.org/10.1523/JNEUROSCI.2580-15.2015

37 New study shows we work harder when we are happy. (2014, March 21). Retrieved March 23, 2017, from https://www2.warwick.ac.uk/newsandevents/pressreleases/new_study_shows/

38 Stone, P. (2013, March 1). *Opting out: Challenging stereotypes and creating real options for women in the professions.* Lecture presented at Gender and Work: Challenging Conventional Wisdom in Harvard Business School, Boston, Massachusetts.

39 Volpp, K. G., John, L. K., Troxel, A. B., Norton, L., Fassbender, J., Loewenstein, G. (2008). Financial incentive–based approaches for weight loss: A randomized trial. *JAMA, 300*(22): 2631–2637. doi:10.1001/jama.2008.804

ABOUT THE AUTHOR

Amy Vetter is an accomplished business executive, serial entrepreneur, national speaker, CPA, and yoga instructor. Throughout her twenty-plus years in business, Amy has learned lessons about how to live an authentic, innovative life in business by creating work-life harmony.

She's a third-generation woman entrepreneur with diverse experience including owning and operating her own accounting practice, yoga studios, and other business ventures. Amy is an advocate and evangelist for entrepreneurship and the accounting profession. She has inspired thousands of business owners, corporate leaders, and accounting professionals as a keynote speaker on business, financial, and technology topics at hundreds of conferences and universities throughout the United States and internationally.

Amy is a corporate executive who has held leadership roles overseeing customer programs, sales, education, and marketing functions. Along with her executive role, she is currently the owner and founder of DRISHTIQ yoga, a studio that she operates with over 50 classes per week, including online yoga services.

Amy was named one of the Most Powerful Women in Accounting in 2016 by *CPA Practice Advisor*, one of the Top 100 Most Influential People for two years in a row by *Accounting Today*, and was selected twice for the Outstanding 40 under 40 list by *CPA Technology Advisor*. She has also been nominated as one of the "Women to Watch" by the California Society of CPAs.

Amy often contributes her best practices and unique insights on entrepreneurship, technology, and the accounting industry to *Entrepreneur, Inc.*, *CPA Practice Advisor*, and *AccountingWEB*. She lives with her husband and two sons in Ohio. Learn more about Amy on her website at www.amyvetter.com.